God
Stephanie

Life As A Single Mom
It Isn't Easy, Or Is It?

10 Steps for Achieving
Success As A Single Mom
and a Compilation of
Heartfelt, Inspiring Stories
Shared by Single Moms

Matthew 19:26
N. Taylor

By Stephanie M. Clark

MDK MEDIA, INC.

Published by MDK Media, Inc.
1086 Livingston Avenue
North Brunswick, NJ 08902
www.mdkmediainc.com
publishing@mdkmediainc.com

Cover Photo: Shabu
Photography by Nicole Lucas
Edited by Sibylla Nash, Sharmonique Shade &
        Ishana Wieczerzak
Proofread by Vernell Dubose & TJ Dupree
DVD Videography by Will Caldwell
        Profile Video Productions, Inc.
Project Assistants: Suphronia Watts, Krystal Brown,
        Frankie Bell & Samantha Wilson

Library of Congress Control Number: 2007907819

ISBN 978-1-60402-447-0

Published in the United States of America
Printed in USA - First Edition

SPECIAL DEDICATIONS

This book is dedicated to my mother Elsie L. Robertson
who single-handedly raised 13 children as a single mom,
without welfare and yes, we all have the same father. LOL
I also dedicate this book to my beloved sister
Cynthia Marie Glover who departed this world in 2004.
She was an exceptional mother and role-model.
To my sisters Diane & Linda, my nieces Tracie, Keelie &
Katreena. You are all exceptional Single Moms and I Love You.

And to my beautiful, brilliant daughter Daphne, I Love You.
Thank you for making my Single Mom journey easy. Never
stop pursuing your dreams. You will always be my
SUPERSTAR!
Thank you for inspiring me to start My Daughter's Keeper.
And, yes, I truly do love you and like you!

A VERY SPECIAL THANK YOU TO OUR SINGLE MOMS
WHO CONTRIBUTED THEIR STORIES TO THIS INSPIRING AND
EMPOWERING BOOK EXPERIENCE

Acknowledgments

In all things I do, I first and foremost want to acknowledge God...just because He Is...no justification required. Since the inception of My Daughter's Keeper, Inc. in 2002, I have had the distinguished pleasure and honor to meet and work with so many wonderful mothers, both married and single who have blessed and enlightened me by sharing their personal trials and triumphs raising their daughters. I have been touched, inspired and have grown as a woman and single mother through my interactions and observations.

To my daughter, Daphne, who inspired the birth of My Daughter's Keeper. Without you there would be no My Daughter's Keeper. I am so grateful to God for gifting you into my life and for giving me the foresight to listen and take seriously your words when you cried out to me that evening, "Mom, I know you love me, but do you like me?" I was forever changed by those words and our relationship has never been stronger.

To my extended daughters: Dana, Sade', CeNedra & Maureen. You are wonderful examples of productive young women. To all of my daughters, and every young lady whom I have had the pleasure of meeting through our programs the past 5 years. I encourage you to never give up and to know that Ms. Stephanie cares and loves each of you dearly. A very special shout out to my daughters at Isaiah's House, the DOVES and

Hayes Residential programs. You know who you are. Keep your eyes and heart focused on your future.

A special thanks to the Board of Trustees of My Daughter's Keeper, Inc. (Dana Williams, Barbara George Johnson, Frankie Bell, LeShawn Anderson, Annette Hale, Jennifer Smith, and Linda Zeigler). Thank you for your dedication and support in helping to make My Daughter's Keeper a national force to be reckoned with and the premier organization of its kind. A special thanks to MDK's therapists who do tremendous work helping to mend the hearts and relationships of mothers, daughters and families: Myrna Torres, LSW; Dr. Gail Reynolds, MSW, LCSW; Cindy Hause, LSW; and Laverne Austin, MSW, LCSW. Much gratitude, love and appreciation to Maria Bruno for keeping a roof over our heads and for being my personal guardian angel. To my church family, the Light of the World Family Worship Church and Pastor Leo & Sister Glynis Sherard, your prayers and support is truly appreciated. To my sister-friends: Regina Chamberlain, Phyllis Cunningham, Sondra Stovall, Carole Dortch-Wright, and Ishana Wieczerzak. Thank you for your love and support!

A special thank you to Sibylla Nash, Sharmonique Shade & Vernell Dubose for offering your editing services to this project. Thank you Will Caldwell, Nicole Lucas, Shanice Williams, Suphronia Watts, and Samantha Wilson for having my back, EVERY TIME! Women who have inspired me from afar: Terrie M. Williams, The Stay Strong Foundation & Joi Gordon, Dress for Success Worldwide. Thank you for EVERYTHING.

CONTENTS

FORWARD

By Elsie L. Robertson
(My Mom)

My husband died in 1969 from a massive heart attack and stroke. A life of partying and drinking led to his leaving this earth at the ripe age of 46.

I had eleven out of thirteen children at home when their father died. I was now a 44-year-old widow who was now the primary financial and emotional caregiver for my children.

I was born in Houston, Texas as the seventh out of 11 children. I was a quiet, reserve girl who was very active in my church. I met my husband at church and married at the tender age of 16. It was the 1940's and many folks were migrating from the South to the Midwestern and Northern states seeking better job opportunities. My husband and I left Texas headed to Gary, Indiana.

A family member offered my husband a better job opportunity in Detroit, Michigan and we relocated from Gary to Detroit a year later with our first and eldest son.

Back in the day, it was customary for wives not to work and to stay at home to care for the children. So, I took on the traditional role as homemaker and tended to my husband, my home, and many babies that would soon follow. We had a total of thirteen children. I was a good mother and took care of my children's needs while my husband worked to provide for us.

My husband liked to hang out after work and enjoyed drinking. I believe his excessive drinking and working long, hard hours led to his early death.

We didn't have the perfect marriage, but it was acceptable. There were times though that I thought I could no longer tolerate his staying out late, drinking, cheating with other women and verbal abuse. I wanted to get out of the marriage. I wasn't working so I knew I would not be able to care for the children and myself if I decided to leave. I knew I could never walk away from my kids so I dealt with the situation.

There were a few occasions when my husband would return home drunk, irate and ready to take out his frustrations on me. A few times he raised his hand to strike me but was blocked by my teenage sons who vowed that they would never let him hit their mother. I tried to keep my children out of the middle of our spousal disagreements.

However, there was one occasion when my husband came home late and drunk and walked in and struck me across my face for no reason at all. The force of his fist hitting my face knocked my eyeglasses across the room to the floor.

I walked away quietly to the kitchen. All I could think and feel was that I don't deserve this and this would be the last time I would allow him to put his hands on me causing pain. I looked around the kitchen counter, not sure what I was looking for. My eyes focused in on a Coca-Cola glass bottle. I grabbed the bottle and walked out of the kitchen into the living room area where my husband was now sitting. I remember standing outside of the French doors that separated the living room from the dining room. I didn't quite enter the living room. I called to my husband in a very soft-spoken voice to come to me. As he walked toward the dining room and passed through the French doors, I stepped from behind the door and struck him in the head with the Coca-Cola bottle. When I saw blood shooting from his head, I ran out of the house down the street screaming and crying hysterically to my neighbor's house. I didn't know what the outcome of my actions would be, but I knew I had to get away from the house just in case he decided to come after me.

My neighbor called the police and they arrived at my home with the paramedics who were dressing my husband's wound. He survived the Coke bottle upside his head.

Back in the day, when the police were called to the house for a domestic disturbance, the police knew that the husband had done something to the wife to cause her to retaliate. My husband told them what I did to him and they asked him what did he do to me first. The police recommended that my husband leave the house for a few hours so that I could return home and cool down. They also recommended that when he returned he should come back begging for my forgiveness for hitting me. They threatened to lock him up if he tried to retaliate or hit me again.

He did return back home, I forgave him and we went back to our lives doing things as normal. Shortly after that incident, I recall thinking to myself while cooking dinner that I needed to do more with my life so that I was not so dependent on my husband.

There had been many times when my husband would come home mad at me for no reason and then give his entire paycheck to one of my daughters to go shopping. He knew that he could make me feel inferior or humiliated when he would do this.

One day while riding on the bus I saw a sign that said "Register for Beauty College." I decided that it was time for me to do something for myself. I needed $100 to register but knew my husband would not give me the money nor support me going to school.

I told my eldest daughter that I wanted to go to school but didn't know how to come up with the registration fee. She told me that she and her husband would pay for me to go to school.

I registered and started going to classes despite the opposition I received from my husband. He threatened me and told me that I better not neglect my responsibilities to him or my children or else I would have to quit beauty school.

I knew I had to go to school for me and my children. He wouldn't allow me to study when he was home so, after he fell asleep, I would hide in the bathroom to do my homework and study.

Somehow I managed to handle all of my responsibilities at home including cooking three meals a day, washing, cleaning, and caring for eleven children while studying and going to beauty school for 18 months. I probably got 2-3 hours of sleep each night. Sometimes I would stay up all night studying while he slept and then go prepare breakfast and get the kids ready for school, just so I could keep the peace.

By the grace of God and my unwavering commitment to myself and my children, I completed beauty school. After graduation, I worked at a beauty salon and saved money to rent a building space, which was only three doors from my home, to open my own beauty salon. Although my husband didn't approve, for some reason he didn't try to stop me from pursuing my goal. There were many days he would come to the salon and I would hold my breath and pray that he wouldn't start an argument or become disruptive before my customers. He realized that this was a dream that he could not take away from me. I was now self-employed, making my own money and contributing to my household.

Three months later my husband died. While I never doubted that I would be able to raise my eleven children alone, who were still at home, other people did.

I remember my mother calling me from Houston after the

funeral and saying, "You may think that you are left alone to raise your children, but you are not alone. Just remember that God is always with you and He will help you raise your children."

The day after my husband's funeral, I received a visit from a man from the Child Welfare department. I was skeptical about letting him into my home because I didn't call them. We sat down at the table and he began to tell me that someone had contacted their office to notify them that my husband had passed and that I had eleven children at home with the youngest being my 2-year-old baby daughter Stephanie as well as a physically and mentally challenged teenage son. He went on to tell me that they wanted to set me up on welfare to receive government assistance to help care for my children.

I immediately interrupted him and told him that I didn't call them and that I didn't need nor want their welfare assistance. He went on to try to convince me why I should accept government assistance and I went on to convince him that I didn't want it or need it.

My children didn't need any clothes because neighbors and my church purchased hundreds of dollars of clothing for my children. They purchased so much food that I had to give some of it away because I didn't have a place to store it.

I told him that I had my own business and that I am able to work and take care of my children. After about an hour, he finally gave up and asked me if there was any way they might be able to help me. He asked me if they could purchase a new stove, refrigerator, washer and dryer. I did accept those items since the ones we had were old. I thank God that I never had to accept welfare to help me raise my children. As long as I was abled-bodied, I was determined and happy to provide for my family on my own.

About a week after my husband's funeral, I was riding on the bus headed to the Social Security Office. There was a woman sitting on the bus in the row in front of me. She was weeping uncontrollably. I felt really sorry for her so I put my hand on her shoulder and asked her what was wrong. She said, "My husband died last week and left me with two kids to raise by myself. I don't know how I'm supposed to raise them on my own. I feel like driving the three of us into the lake." I said to her, "Oh, please don't do that. My husband died last week too and I have eleven children at home to raise alone." She looked up at me in amazement and said, "If I were you I would jump off the bridge if I had all those children to raise by myself." I told her that my children were a gift from God and that God chose to take my husband instead of me because He knew that I would not give up on my children and that I would be the stronger parent should I have to raise my children alone. I went on to tell her that she was stronger than she thought and that God left the children in her care to raise because He trusted that she would be the stronger parent. She dried her eyes and said to me, "I never thought about it that way."

The bus arrived at my stop and as I was getting off to go into the Social Security Office, the lady got off too. We both were going to the same place. She asked if it was alright if she sat next to me in the office. I told her I didn't mind. She thanked me and smiled as we walked through the doors together.

As my children grew older, the older ones would take care of the younger ones while I worked at the beauty salon. I took my youngest daughter and physically-challenged son to work with me. I fixed up the back room in my salon so that they could have a comfortable place to stay while I worked in the front room.

My children were my number one priority. I worked hard to make sure we kept a roof over our heads and food on the table. I was the mother and father for my children. I didn't have any family in Detroit to help me raise my children, but then it was not my family's responsibility to raise my children. I gave birth to my thirteen children and accepted the responsibility of raising them the best that I could. My children didn't get everything they wanted, but they had what they needed. I shopped at Kresges and Woolworth discount stores. There were no name brands in my house, but my children never went to school with dirty clothes or hungry bellies. We didn't have a lot, but we had enough. If one child had money to buy a dollar bag of cookies, he or she would be sure to share with the others.

I raised my children in church. On Sunday mornings, there would be at least 10 of us waiting at the bus stop to catch our ride to church.

Although my children were my life, I did date occasionally. However, I never brought a man home to my bed or around my children. I was never looking for a man to become my children's father.

After several of my children became grown and moved out, I met and dated one man seriously for several years. He was a good man and respected my wishes to protect my children. He never stayed overnight and always brought me home at respectable hours. He was good to my children. Although I cared a great deal for him, we never married.

I am extremely proud of my daughter Stephanie for the wonderful job she has done as a single mother. I really appreciate the opportunity to be a part of this special book. I wish her continued success in all that she does and pray that God will continue to strengthen, direct her path, and bless her abundantly for serving others.

My words of wisdom and encouragement to the single moms who read this book are that you can do it! Make your children your number one priority. Love them through your actions and not just your words. You are stronger than you think you are.

I pray God's blessings over you and your children.

Meet Our Mother of 13 Children
Elsie L. Robertson

Meet the Single Moms in My Family
(L-R) My eldest sister Rev. Diane Covington; my
niece Tracie Rasberry, my sister Linda Davis and
my niece Keelie Robertson; and me and my
beloved sister Cynthia Glover

INTRODUCTION

Driving a truck that says, "My Daughter's Keeper," is great advertising but sometimes attracts unexpected attention. Here is a case in point. While dropping my daughter off at school one evening for her spring musical, a woman (who happened to be a single mom), sees my truck and suddenly jumps inside crying hysterically about her teenage daughter who has been lying and being disrespectful to her.

"Being a single mom isn't easy," is something I hear constantly over and over throughout my travels and I mostly hear it from people who are not single moms. It sometimes feels like they pity me and other single moms. As I recollect back to past instances of when I have heard someone say that "being a single mom isn't easy," generally I agree with them. However, for some reason, although I agree with those words, they have never truly resonated within me and I find myself pondering the question why isn't it easy?

When I think about my daughter Daphne, I often say to myself, "You have really done a great job raising her as a single mom." My daughter is not perfect but, my God, she's near it. I don't compare her to the daughter of anyone else, and I don't compare my life as a single mom to any other single mom either.

As I reflect on being a single mom for fifteen years, looking at my daughter and seeing how she has developed into such a beautiful, productive and healthy young lady, I can honestly say to myself that being a single mom has been easy for me.

It is not that I haven't gone through trials and tribulations. But, all the trials and tribulations I have experienced in my life, whether it has been relationships, finances (usually lack of), and my divorce had nothing to do with me being a single mom. They had more to do with me being a woman, an African American woman and my responses to the hard issues of life. Such as, when I had the unpleasant experience of being discriminated against by an employer, or when I made poor choices in men or unwise financial decisions. My struggles have never really been as a result of being a single mom, but rather, choices I have made as a woman. This is why I have written this book. I want to empower single moms by giving them the tools to become fulfilled single women. And I want to enlighten people who tend to pity single moms and automatically give us the disclaimer that if you are a single mom, you are going to have hardships, more struggles with your children, and not be able to raise a healthy, productive child by yourself. WE CAN DO IT!

My life as a single mom and the stories shared by the other single moms in this book will hopefully dispel many of the myths about single moms. Through this book, you will read about the journey of other single moms who agree with the phrase that "being a single mom is not easy, but it is worth it!"

I will share some steps to achieving success as a single woman and single mom, as well as strategies I use and coach other mothers to use to have a healthier relationship with their daughters. The things I talk about in this book are what I do and practice on a daily basis with raising my daughter.   I will share some of the things that I have done, decisions I have made and the thought process that I have gone through to help me make the most effective choices for my daughter. My desire is to inspire single moms and mothers in general who may read this book. For those single moms who pity themselves and seek pity from others to try to better their situations...STOP IT!

Just because we are single moms does not mean we are not or cannot become successful women and parents. Yes, we will encounter some struggles. However, keep in mind that there are many married couples struggling with a two-family income to make ends meet. And, many married households have problems raising their children. Just watch "Supernanny."

One of my goals for this book is to get single moms to stop setting themselves up for failure as parents because they have bought into what society says about us; that we cannot be effective parents and raise productive, healthy children if there is not a father in the picture. We are resilient, most of us. So we must encourage society to stop pitying us and to stop stereotyping all single moms as mothers who are on welfare, with five or six children and unable to adequately take care of them. Okay, I will admit that there are some women out there who fit into this category, but they are not the norm for single moms.

For the single mom who has chosen to use being a single mom as an excuse for not being a productive woman who makes wise choices for the betterment of herself and her children, I encourage you to start believing in yourself and stop allowing society to label you. Once you begin to truly value your worth as a woman first, not just as a single mom, you will be able to understand what is necessary to take care of yourself and your children. No longer will you allow society to dictate how successful you can be raising your children.

So, being a single mom is not easy or is it? Well, that is for each single mom to determine, not society.

PROJECT SINGLE MOMS CONTRIBUTORS

"Our deepest fear is not that we are inadequate. Our deepest fear is that we are powerful beyond measure. It is our light, not our darkness, that frightens us most. We ask ourselves, 'Who am I to be brilliant, gorgeous, talented, and famous?' Actually, who are you not to be? You are a child of God. Your playing small does not serve the world. There is nothing enlightened about shrinking so that people won't feel insecure around you. We were born to make manifest the glory of God that is within us. It's not just in some of us; it's in all of us. And when we let our own light shine, we unconsciously give other people permission to do the same. As we are liberated from our own fear, our presence automatically liberates others."

Marianne Williamson (spiritual mentor)

Chapter One

HOW TO DISTINGUISH YOURSELF FROM WOMAN AND SINGLE MOM

Being a Woman and being a single mom are two very distinct roles and you really have to be able to define who you are as a woman first and foremost. If you understand who you are as a woman it will impact who you will become as a single mom, not the other way around. Being a single mom should not define who you are as a woman. We are women first. When God created us He created man and He created WOMAN, not man and single moms. Now, I do not believe that most single moms choose to be single, but some do, depending on the circumstances. Although I truly wanted to remain married for a lifetime, I chose to become a single mom in order to escape the verbal abuse and never-ending unhappiness I experienced while married. As single moms, we need to understand what our needs are and how they differ from our needs as women.

Once we understand what our needs are as women, it should enable us to gain clarity and focus so we can learn to prioritize our specific responsibilities as single moms.

We need to talk about and define what our needs are as a woman. What are your needs?

My Needs as a Woman Are: (List your needs)

_____

_____

_____

_____

_____

_____

_____

_____

_____

_____

_____

_____

_____

_____

_____

_____

_____

_____

Having children is only one need or one desire of a woman. We may desire to have an education. We may desire to be married. We may desire to start our own businesses. We may even desire to become the next American Idol!

If Fantasia Barrino can do it, why not you? Being a mother is only one of the options we choose as women.

My Needs as a Single Mom Are: (List your needs)

_____

_____

_____

_____

_____

_____

_____

_____

_____

_____

_____

_____

_____

_____

_____

_____

_____

_____

Let us talk a moment about the choices we make as women. I can personally attest that I have made some unwise choices in my lifetime and, unfortunately, probably will make a few more. It is all part of living and learning and we will never grow too old to continue learning and growing as individuals.

On the other hand, I have made some very wise choices in my lifetime as well. Actually, most of the unwise choices I have made, I made them as a woman using her free-will to make decisions that ultimately impacted my life in a positive or negative way. I would like to share some of the unwise choices I have made as a woman with you. For starters, I made many unwise choices in selecting men and it was probably an unwise choice for me to marry at the young, tender age of 22. I have made unwise choices with my finances. I am sure I could have spent less and saved more over the years as well as done a better job prioritizing my financial needs and wants. I know that I have made unwise choices with my health and unfortunately continue to do so. These are all unwise choices I have freely and willfully made. I have made far more unwise choices as a woman than I have made as a single mom. I am not perfect, still working on myself, growing as a woman and learning how to make wiser life choices.

I feel it truly is a blessing that I have been able to make wise choices as a single mom when it came to making decisions raising my daughter. I am very fortunate that I have managed to raise a healthy, brilliant, beautiful and productive daughter on my own. While there have been times when I questioned whether or not I was making the best decision as a parent as I tried to steer her in the right direction, the outcomes of my efforts are made evident each and every time someone compliments me on how wonderful, sweet, well-mannered, considerate, and smart my daughter is. I did not always take credit for the young lady she has developed into because I have always believed and known that I have not raised my daughter totally alone. I acknowledge the role that God has played in both our lives, but particularly my life as a single mom for I realize that I could not have done such a great job raising her without much prayer and faith. Also, I trusted that God would equip me with the tools and foresight I needed to instill within her the necessary morals and values. I also prayed, asking Him for guidance and wisdom to use my better judgment when making decisions as a single mom that would ultimately impact and shape the person she develops into. I recognize that I am not the perfect parent, but I am proud of myself for producing my greatest accomplishment, my daughter.

When my daughter and I relocated to New Jersey in 1998, I did question whether or not I was making the wisest decision in uprooting my daughter from our family and moving her to an unfamiliar place where we had no family, at all.

Time has proven that as a single mom, relocating was a very wise choice I made for both of us. My daughter has flourished as a young lady. She has been exposed to many cultures and opportunities, which is something I feared she would not have received had I chosen not to relocate.

We are often confronted with many challenges and decisions that we must make both as a woman and single mom. In most cases, we tend to put the needs and well-being of our children before our own. We make sacrifices and do without so that our children do not feel the impact of the unwise choices we sometimes make as women who are dedicated and loving single moms.

The most important thing to know is that the choices we make as women (wise or unwise) help to shape us into stronger, more resilient women and influence the persons our children will grow up to become.

Take a moment to reflect on the unwise choices you may have made in areas of your life as a woman invoking her free-will. Then, indicate how you have grown and what you have learned about yourself as a result of experiencing the consequences of your unwise choices.

_____

_____

_____

_____

_____

_____

_____

_____

_____

_____

_____

_____

_____

_____

_____

_____

Now, reflect on the unwise choices you may have made as a single mom that had an impact on your child (ren). Indicate how you have grown and what you have learned about yourself as a result of experiencing the consequences of your unwise choices.

_____

_____

_____

_____

_____

_____

_____

_____

_____

_____

_____

_____

_____

_____

The challenges faced by women who are single-handedly rearing their children can be overwhelming. I want you to know that you are not alone. Be encouraged as you read these stories by single moms who openly share their hearts and experiences with you.

_____

"My biggest challenge as a single mom was embracing my own problems first as a woman (i.e. recovery from alcohol, drugs, co-dependency, food addiction, gambling, etc.) while attempting to raise my children. I was blessed to have had a college degree and with that came better employment opportunities."

Anita Yasin, New Jersey

"My greatest challenge as a woman and a single mom has been not having the balance of a parental and personal partnership. It is difficult to lay your head down at night and not have the support of a partner to discuss life's events with."

Charisse Roberts, New Jersey

"As a woman, finding the time to be a good mother to three children while working full-time and trying to get back in school is something that I struggle with daily. Taking on the challenges of excelling in motherhood, needing to finish my education to begin my career, keeping up with my family and friends - sometimes I feel that no matter how much I give, it's not enough."

Danlia Reyes, New York

"My greatest challenge as a woman has been accepting the fact that I am a single mother. I guess in the beginning I was in denial, but when the reality hit, it hit me hard."

Darlene Morgan, New York

"I believe that what you think, you will become. I take my role as a mother to be one of most important characteristics of who I am. It's not important that people know me as Dr. Nelson, what inspires me is when someone gives me a compliment and says "You have done a fine job with your girls."

Gayle Nelson, PhD, New Jersey

"As a woman, making the right decision to have my daughters and to raise them even if it meant raising them as a single mother was a great challenge for me. The day they entered into this world, it was about loving and teaching them to become respectful young ladies and instilling in them values and morals.

It was an effort staying positive and sacrificing to make ends meet even though there were many difficulties relating to family, friends, community, and unhealthy relationships that sometimes made me think that things weren't possible for me to achieve. I really didn't have past accomplishments but past failures. However, the past fifteen years have been an experience and a great transformation just to live and have faith for today."

La-trenda Ross, New Jersey

"Being a single mom does not mean that as a woman I am somehow less of a person because I am raising a child alone. I know that children are a gift and having my daughter is one of the greatest joys of my life."

Miriam Parrotto, New Jersey

"As a woman, it seems like new challenges are presented as time goes by. In general, I think I am consistently faced with finding the right balance between the responsibilities of my job vs. spending time with my daughter; providing emotional support while still seeking my own emotional and spiritual nurturing; being a best friend and disciplinarian. In addition to the balancing act, I find myself suffering from "mommy guilt." From the time I went back to work to the present, I have always felt guilt for what I have been able to provide in regards to time, experience and emotional support. When my daughter was a baby, I always felt guilty about not spending enough time with her. So, when I came home from work, instead of putting her to bed at 8:00 like most babies, I kept her up so we could spend time together. To this day she goes to bed way too late and can't get up in the morning. I feel guilty because financially I can't provide her with some of the things I had as a child like a house with a yard (I own my condo but it's not the same). I feel guilty about making bad decisions when it comes to my own relationships with men and I have yet to find the man that can serve as a constant father figure in her life."

Monique Lawton, New Jersey

"Working my own business and being able to work a commission-based position as an independent contractor has been a great accomplishment. It has allowed me to be available for my children when they needed me to be. When my ex-husband left, he was not consistent in the children's lives and it did affect them tremendously. I had to learn quickly how to balance work and home with little-to-no monetary support coming from their father for some time before it became consistent. My greatest accomplishments have been to work all the hours that I do and still maintain 'happy and healthy' children."

Robyn Lynn Blocker, New Jersey

"It's become so hard lately to maintain my home, continue my education, stay on point at work, and serve as much as I want to at church. I'm learning balance right now and setting priorities, recognizing that I'm unable to do everything. I have to definitely keep my daughter on the top of the list, but at times I believe I allow everything to become so overwhelming and then it seems as if she's definitely affected by that. I started to include her in all the areas of my life. When I'm at work she's in school, so when I leave work I try to leave work at work. I'm serving as a youth leader at church, so she is involved in that ministry as well. I need a second job badly, so I'm thinking of starting my own business, something that she could also be involved in."

Shanick Moore, New Jersey

"I had my first child when I was 14 and my third and last at 21. When my children were younger, my greatest challenge was supporting them financially. I think my greatest personal challenge was trying to balance being a very young person with being a very young single mom. The truth is there were things that I wanted to do because I was young but being a mother meant that I had to prioritize and sometimes delay personal gratification. I often worked on my feelings about the pressure of not being able to function as a traditional teen. The fact that I was not a "traditional" mom added to the degree of pressure too. It was difficult at times. Now that my children are older, finances are an issue but our communication is the greatest challenge. They are 17, 19, and 23 now and I find myself wishing they would talk more, but they are just all so busy."

Simone Bellamy, New Jersey

"As a woman, it is a challenge trying to maintain a business but, as a single mom, it is important for me to teach my daughters how to depend on themselves and be successful without a man while allowing God to lead their lives.

I graduated college with a double major, establishing a small construction business. Although we have not made any money this year, gaining self-respect (I had low self-esteem for a long time) was a great accomplishment for me.

I wish that I knew that God deserves all of the glory and not to put my heart and soul into a relationship that will bring me down. I owe some of my success to my husband because he brought me down emotionally, physically, mentally and spiritually; but, when I let go and let God I realized that God has prepared me through my husband to become a stronger woman. I also wish that I knew I was beautiful and wanted and that God had a plan for me. I wish that my self-esteem wasn't an issue back then and it sometimes plays a part now."

Anonymous

"My greatest challenge has been balancing my daughters' needs as a single mom and my needs as a woman. My greatest accomplishments are my three beautiful daughters; they are extremely respectful, caring, responsible and helpful young ladies. They are all good girls who strive to do their best.

In the early years as a parent, I tried to be a superwoman. Over the years I've learned that it's ok not to be perfect. I wish I had known back in the day that it was ok to let the clothes pile up or to let dishes stay in the sink overnight. I'm comfortable with who and what I am, a single mom raising three healthy girls to be independent and self-sufficient.

I tell my girls all the time that we are able to have so much fun together because I had a life before them and I don't feel as if I'm missing out on anything. I experienced a lot of things and waited to have my girls. I got to hang out and see the world because I didn't have children. I stress that waiting and completing things that you want in life will make having children more fun."

Tracie Rasberry, Michigan

Chapter Two

MOVING FROM PITY TO PROSPERITY

"I certainly don't regret my experiences because without them,
I couldn't imagine who or where I would be today. Life is an
amazing gift to those who have overcome great obstacles,
and attitude is everything!"

Sasha Azevedo

Society typically labels single moms as weak, ineffective parents because we don't have husbands. And, more often than not, single moms are disqualified especially if you're raising sons. According to some, a single mom is ill-equipped to successfully raise a son, but we know that is not true. There are plenty of single moms who are now raising, or have successfully raised, productive sons and daughters.

We first need to learn how to eliminate self-pity from our lives. One of the ways to do this is by not allowing society to label or pity you. Society comes in all shapes and sizes. Your society may include your parents, siblings, employers, educational system, social services, media, government and others.

We need to re-educate society and really give new meaning to how society chooses to define single moms. Single mothers are resourceful. We are creative. We are survivors. We are nurturers. We are educated. We are financially secure. We are many things. And that's because before we were single moms, we were women. We are women with great goals, dreams and accomplishments. We can no longer allow society to label us as lazy, baby-making machines who lack the motivation to successfully raise our children because we run a single-parent household. Women are strong; therefore, single moms are strong and can become stronger.

Some single moms in their weakened state, whether it is because of poor health, bad relationships, or that they feel like they have to over compensate so much for their children in the absence of their fathers, tend to pity themselves. My plea to these single moms is to RECLAIM YOUR POWER. We need to understand our power and position.

There are many successful single moms. Some of the most notable single moms include TV personality Katie Couric, Actress, singer Vanessa Williams, and American Idol winner Fantasia Barrino, just to name a few. There are also many unknown single moms who may not possess the wealth and resources of the celebrity single moms mentioned. Although parenting alone, they work hard through challenges they may encounter while raising emotionally and physically healthy children into productive adults.

I know firsthand that there are days when we (single moms) may feel overwhelmed, alone and ready to throw in the towel. But, we know that we cannot give in because we have our children, and in many cases, others such as our elderly parents, employers, clients, places of worship counting on us to be strong and make it happen without skipping a beat.

I will admit that there are times when I allow myself to have a pity party. I don't generally invite anyone to join me because I don't allow my pity party to last for more than 30 minutes. As a leader and someone who others look up to and turn to for help and support, I often feel alone because I do not have anyone I can turn to for support and strength. Therefore, I give myself permission to retreat to a place of solitude and commence to lose myself in pity. Before I enter this place, I tell myself you can cry, scream at the top of your lungs, jump up and down, even knock something over (as long as it is not valuable or breakable) for no more than 30 minutes. Then, I get over it and move on for "weeping may endure for a night, but joy cometh in the morning" - Psalm 30:5.

Life does get hard at times. We can only do our best and trust that our current circumstances or situations will soon pass and know that better days are yet ahead. We must not allow ourselves to give up or give in. We cannot become lost or consumed with pity for ourselves or over our situations. "But in all these things we are more than conquerors through him who loved us" - Romans 8:37.

There is a song that says "Your latter will be greater than your past." When I am feeling discouraged or overwhelmed, I remember these words. I interpret these words to mean that my latter days to come will be filled with many blessings and prosperity. I will reflect back on my past challenges as a single mom and rejoice knowing that my trials only came to make me a stronger person and to prepare me for the greatness that shall come during my latter days. I am walking into my latter days as I write this book which means I am walking toward God's promise that He would prosper me beyond my most unimaginable dreams as a result of enduring my life's challenges and remaining steadfast in my faith and obedience to fulfill God's call on my life.

Single moms, I implore you to remain faithful and focused on the tasks at hand and your latter days will soon be greater than your past.

These courageous single moms share their stories about how they have triumphed over pity in their lives to prosper as single moms.

"I advise all single parents to continue to enjoy life WITH your children. Face your fears of being alone and look for spiritual strength by any means necessary. Your connection to life comes through your family, so never lose it or forget to enjoy every moment of it: the good, bad, happy and sad. Create beautiful memories early so you teach them how to enjoy what they have through you. Do not allow yourself to feel deprived or denied because where there is a will there is a way. Love comes from different people, places and things that God sends you towards."

Anita Yasin, New Jersey

"I am smiling, beaming and walking around proud because I know it was through my dedication, hard work, parenting style and perseverance that my daughter's accolades arise. Her praises are all a direct result of her mother. I aim to always dispel the myth that a single-parent household can be a disadvantage for a child. If anything, that myth has made me more determined in raising a well-rounded, well-mannered, educated and beautiful daughter."

Carla Alexander, New Jersey

"I was tired of raising my child alone, tired and ready to give up when one day my three-year-old daughter looked at me and said, "I want my old mommy back!" The stress that I was under was undeniable and my daughter could see it in me. I had to change. That was a wake-up call for me that I needed to change my life. I needed to stop worrying about how my job was treating me and how my ex wasn't doing his part. The idea of losing the home that I worked so hard to obtain was a challenge I didn't want to face. I knew I had to figure out a plan because I moved a lot when I was a child and I wanted to provide a loving, stable environment in a community with good schools and a happy place for my daughter and myself. I worked long hours and there was no time for dating or serious relationships. The hard work finally paid off when I worked my way out of foreclosure, my debt was mostly paid off, and I received a promotion on my job. But, the most important accomplishment for me is being able to have my daughter look at me and see me happy, making good choices, and removing the stress from my life."

Cassandra White Graves, Ohio

"When your life has fallen apart like mine had, you have to make a choice. Either you give up and sink into a depression or you muster up any slight glimmer of hope and forge on. I chose to fight back. I had four innocent children who needed me. So, I gathered whatever little strength I had left inside of me."

Christina Rowe, Florida

"It is very challenging to be only one person playing two significant roles. Nevertheless, I have been able to stand on my own two feet, excel in my work and in the community, and go back to college. I have accomplished so much throughout my trials and challenges, but I have high goals and I have so much to be accountable for when it comes to my daughters."

Jeanine Fuller, Tennessee

"Getting back on my feet with two children after a bad divorce was a challenge I triumphed over. My husband put me and my 7-year-old out of the house when I was four months pregnant with my second child. We had just relocated to Virginia for his job, I had given up a $50,000 job to relocate and become a homemaker. When he put us out I had nothing, I drove back to

New Jersey with $200.00 in my pocket. I was forced to live with relatives for a year and a half and to get on welfare (which I had never done before). A month after I had my daughter I worked a temporary job (and got off welfare) until I was able to find a full-time job. I purchased a car and got my own place. I worked hard to get back on my feet."

Kasanu Sims, New Jersey

"Living from paycheck to paycheck is difficult enough, but not being able to do things that are not luxuries but a long-term benefit for your children is a difficult dilemma. Other challenges of single motherhood included being in a situation and really just not knowing what decision to make because the experiences your children have can be out of the ordinary in comparison to your own. Nevertheless, I am proud to say that I have kept a roof over my children's heads and my young people have turned out well. My greatest accomplishment is exhibiting for my children that getting things done is possible."

Laticia Bailey, New Jersey

"My greatest challenges as a single mom have been combating the effects of domestic violence on my kids and myself, making major financial decisions and always trying to rectify problems as they occur through counseling and seeking support from organizations designed to help with parenting skills and ways to accept and forgive the perpetrators of domestic violence.

Hearing my kids say things or do things fluently and without thought, knowing they have good morals and ideals and methods that I thought they never picked up from me make me feel as though I have accomplished something with them. They recognize the signs of violence and assault when it confronts them; and, instead of accepting it they move on, having recognized the threats before they become too entrenched in the victim mode. My kids' self-esteem and love for themselves, animals, others, and me is very important.

I believe that women can be successful and survive on their own. We don't need men or others abusing us in our lives. We can stand alone and succeed better than always thinking we have to rely on others in our lives. Seeking help is not a weakness but strength. We don't always have to live the ways of our past when there has been nothing but abuse and we can make the difference. We do have a choice to say 'No' which can be very empowering to realize."

Louise Marie Clayton, Wagga Wagga, Australia

"My daughter's father has gone to great lengths to avoid paying child support over the past 12 years. My goal was to get to a point where I could live comfortably whether or not he paid child support. Even with working, we struggled to get by. I can't tell you how many times my name has been on the eviction dockets in New Jersey. I got my first car when my daughter was seven years old and less than 7 months later I suffered a brain injury in a car accident that changed our lives. I eventually lost my job because I couldn't do it anymore and spent a year unemployed on disability trying to find myself as a single mother with a brain injury. I lost hope and was so afraid of losing my daughter and ending up in an assisted living facility; I had to find help.

Since my accident five years ago, my condition has improved and so did my life. Beginning in January 2007, I reached a level of financial stability. It's still hard to believe, but for the first time, I can sleep at night without wondering how to pay the bills. We can't afford a house, but we live in a very nice apartment in a middle-class neighborhood. Child support is still a problem but we don't starve without it. It is a daily struggle to maintain financial stability, but I am so grateful for what we have. Life as a single mother isn't easy, but it is so worth it!"

Miriam Parrotto, New Jersey

"Not passing the feelings of anger that I had for my soon-to -be ex-husband to my children, regaining financial stability after having lived in a domestic violence shelter and being evicted, managing my sons' anger, and worrying what effect all of it would have on my daughter are some of the ills that haunt me in single motherhood.

I have managed as a single mom to instill faith in my family, having my children perform exceptionally well in school, knowing that even though we may not have the newest of things that we are always clean, and manage to get by with prayer. The effort I put into making my children aware of humility and the importance of having manners shows, and knowing that my children know to whom all honor is due. Last but not least, I am proud when I am having a not-so-good day and they serve as a source of encouragement to me the same way that I encourage them."

Shanda Harris, New Jersey

"My greatest challenge as a single mom has been being homeless with both my baby daughters. It was the greatest challenge I overcame through God's grace and loyalty. My greatest accomplishments as a single mom are that I am tickled pink over having two very beautiful, happy, healthy, and God-loving children, despite all that we have endured.

I am also pleased I can maintain a clean (for the most part), pretty and spacious home on a beautiful street in a nurturing community that's particularly geared for kids. It required us to move three states away from my "home state," but I am so thrilled we did. We relocated to the mountains from a city by the sea. I see my daughters flourishing with flying colors because of my ambitious nature and pro-activity. We have even made the media with our story which is a great accomplishment! I have conquered gigantic obstacles that most persons (let alone - a single mom) will never face. I have kicked homelessness, various addictions, several abuses, the loss of two older children, and the list goes on. I am doing everything I can possibly do to crush the curse of poverty and to turn into a prosperous woman/mom. I keep a clean house and yet let my kids be kids. I try my best to feed my children healthy organic food that's tasty. Perhaps the most important thing I can do for my offspring is guide their spirituality in a Godly manner with a loving approach because their souls are on the line and they need my direction."

Sinneh Rose, Massachusetts

"Right now I am not in the best place in life. Last year my business made $35,000, but it was not due to the business alone. I had to get on welfare and take menial jobs to put food on the table and to pay bills. I am currently past due on more than half of my bills because I cannot find a job and the real estate and construction business is slow. I can't provide for my girls like I want to and I am married to their father who is in jail.

Parenting is absolutely hard. There are great challenges and you must have patience. When times get rough for a parent sometimes the only thing [I] we know how to do is yell at our children. No money in the world can make you a good parent, but all of the patience, praying, understanding, time spent, and nurturing will. God is always the answer for me and once I put Him first, things began to look up for me. That is why I have made some goals and have accomplished some of them.

Let Go and Let God! Prayer does work. Let me tell you, if it hadn't been for God in my life and being saved I don't know where I would be. I've contemplated suicide when my (then) boyfriend cheated on me, abused me, spit in my face and just down right didn't care about me. I thought I was all he needed and he would make me feel better. I know that my past has a lot to do with why I've had low self-esteem, but my future and God has helped me get past that. I know that I can do all things through Christ who strengthens me."

Anonymous

"My greatest challenge has been surviving the horror of 9/11. Shortly after escaping with my life, I found out I was pregnant with my now five- year-old. I wasn't eating or sleeping and I was an emotional mess. My 11-year-old worried more about me than being in school and her grades suffered. There were many days I thought my family would be better off without me. I repeatedly told myself that I would not be able to raise my new baby and that I could not afford her. One night God came to me and said, 'If you have her you will be blessed.' I have always believed and have always prayed. Needless-to-say, my daughter was born and she is happy and healthy. My two children are my greatest accomplishments and a testimony to my spiritual strength."

Tracey Slaughter, New Jersey

Chapter Three

BE A PROACTIVE PARENT, NOT A REACTIVE PARENT

"Whatever they grow up to be, they are still our children, and
the one most important of all the things we can give to them
is unconditional love. Not a love that depends on anything at
all except that they are our children."

Rosaleen Dickson

As single moms, it is important to understand that times
are different. That is to say that many things in our society are
not the same as when we were growing up. Today, a great deal
of emphasis is not placed on protecting the innocence of our
children. Traditional family values have all but disappeared and
many children are left to fend for themselves. In most severe
cases, parents choose not to accept any accountability in rearing
their children, but rather leave it to the school system, law
enforcement or the media. There has to be a safe middle ground
when raising our children. We must recognize that if we have
taken time to truly instill morals and values into our children,
we have to learn to trust them. It is our responsibility to set
appropriate boundaries for our children and let them know that

we have expectations of them. We have to become proactive and not reactive parents.

We need to understand that children need nurturing, discipline and boundaries. When we surrender control and power over to our children to the point where they feel they can take on authoritative roles, they begin to exhibit disrespect not only towards the parent, but toward other adults and persons in authority as well. As single moms, we need not feel as though we should be our child's best friend in order for our children to love us.

Most single moms work full-time jobs. We are always busy and sometimes working two jobs. We cannot be with our children 24-hours a day and we do not always know what is going on with them. As mothers, we have to become insightful and at least be in tune to what is going on in their lives. There are ways for us to do this, such as taking time to get to know the friends our children hang out with. Just because they tell us, "I'm going over Darlene's house, she is in my class or she goes to my school," it should not be acceptable and guarantee them clear entry to make that move. If you have not met Darlene's parents and you do not know who lives in that household, then you should not be so willing to allow your child to go and visit. Do not allow your child to stay overnight at someone's home that you do not know just because they say the person is their friend. We are sometimes too trusting as mothers and we want to believe that our children will always make the right choices. Your child may be a good child, but sometimes our children meet and befriend bad people who they are influenced by to make poor choices. "Bad company corrupts good character." - I Corinthians 15:33.

Oftentimes, our children assume that they do not have any boundaries due to our actions or lack thereof. In their minds they think that, "mom does not care if I leave school and go over to Bartholemew's house even though she has not met his parents or know anything about his family."

We have to learn to be proactive and not wait until our children begin to act out by lying and showing disrespect toward us before we feel that we need to react. Sometimes we don't know how to react because we are caught off guard by the shifts in the behavior of our children. We have to be proactive by making time to do the following:

- Attend parent-teacher conferences to learn how our children are doing in school.
- Meet the parents of their friends and know what type of people they are before you give approval for your child to spend time with them.
- Talk to your children and take time to let them know that they are your number one priority.

We must let them know that not only do we care about their actions, but we are also holding them accountable for taking care of business in school and at home. If you do not have a presence at your child's school, your absence gives them more room to act out or not to be held accountable for going to class and turning in assignments because they know you are not checking in on them.

Here is something to think about that may "tick" a few single moms off, but I am going to say it anyway.

Generally, the parents who make time to go to parent-teacher conferences, attend school activities their children participate in, and inquire about and check homework daily, have children who do well in school and most often, never receive calls from the school's administration.

Parents who do not take the time, or make it a priority to be a proactive participant in their child's education, are generally those parents whose children do not go to class regularly, turn in assignments, and receives the calls from the Principal's office. There is something wrong here and it is not only with the children. If you are falling short of the mark as an effective parent, start today to become proactive and actively involved in your child's school life.

Most children will start to show signs or evidence that something is going on with them; and we must be tuned-in and alert enough to recognize signs when our children may be crying out to us or really trying to get our attention. Sometimes, the way to get our attention is by getting into trouble. They may begin to act in ways that are unfavorable, so we have to learn how to read more into their actions, their attitudes, and their behaviors. Do not just blow off your child's behavior and think that they are just having a bad day, being a brat or acting spoiled.

A minor change in behavior can serve as an early warning sign that there is a problem with your children and they may not be comfortable coming to you to tell you what is going on in their minds and their lives. As single moms, we must be proactive, not feel like we are intruding in their lives, and investigate to find out what is going on. First and foremost, we must remember that we are the parents and they are the children.

These single moms offer some very helpful advice to allow you to respond proactively when parenting your children.

"Always communicate with your children and be a good listener. Stay involved with your children throughout their school years; know their teachers, know their friends, make unannounced visits to the school and provide support for their extracurricular interests and academic endeavors. Do not underestimate your children's creativity and provide opportunities for them to nurture their creativity. Share a good hearty laugh with your children daily. Tell your children that they are beautiful, pray and worship with your children. Depending on the issue, allow your children to attend family meetings to discuss issues. Never assume your children don't understand or you can hide the truth. Assist your children in understanding finances (from allowances to retirement), read and watch television with your children and most importantly love your children unconditionally."

Gayle Nelson, PhD, New Jersey

"Dealing with my children's emotional needs is a great challenge for me. They miss their father's presence on a daily basis. I thought they would be happy for me, not realizing that they missed him being in the home. I have to be aware of addressing their issues instead of allowing them to suffer in silence."

TJ Dupree, New Jersey

Chapter Four

RECLAIM YOUR PARENT POWER!

"If my mind can conceive it, and my heart can believe it,
I know I can achieve it."
Jesse Jackson

Do not forget your place as a parent. It is incredible how many mothers I have spoken with tell me, "My daughter talks to me like she is my mother." And why is that? I ask. Do you allow her to speak to you with disrespect? Have you empowered her to talk to you in such a manner as if she has authority over you? How long have you allowed this behavior to occur?

Most likely this is behavior that has been going on for years and now that your child has stopped listening to you, you are now ready to react as a parent. Remember, you have to be a proactive parent and address the negative behavior when your child first exhibits it. We must know our roles as parents and understand the consequences we may face if we surrender authority to our children. Let me remind you that you are the parent and occasionally you may need to remind your child of this fact.

When dealing with a disobedient, disrespectful child, sometimes situations can get so rough that we may feel like giving up and letting someone else deal with our headaches (our children). In many cases, our first thought may be to let them go live with their father if he is present in their lives. I will admit, when my daughter rubs me the wrong way, more than once I have had that same thought.

Or, we may want to ship them off to some other distant relative that we know probably does not want to be bothered either with the ill-mannered creature we have allowed to manifest. Our out-of-control children are our mess to clean up. It is not the responsibility of the school system, the church, nor the juvenile justice system to raise our children.

You may find it difficult to obtain the strength to begin to reclaim your power and authority over your child(ren), but you can do it. The key is to be consistent in your tone, stance, demeanor, attitude, and disciplinary actions resulting from the misbehavior. When you give a directive or make a request that your child may not be accustomed to hearing from you, be prepared to be challenged; stand your ground and do not waver. It is important that you speak with authority and maintain eye contact with your child when you expect them to adhere to your request.

I have seen single moms succumb to intimidation and in some cases fear of their own children. Refuse to give in to their threats and manipulation. You must realize that you possess the power and strength within to prove to your child(ren) that you are the adult and head of your household. Surrender your spirit of fear, doubt, and weakness and acknowledge that you are the WOMAN of the house. When you begin to reclaim your rightful place and consistently demand respect and control, your children will soon fall in line.

Also, remember that when your children reach the age of 18 or choose to make adult choices such as becoming teenage mothers, it does not give them the right to challenge your authority or feel they no longer need to abide by your rules.

If your adult children choose to reside in your household, their age or bearing a child does not provide them with the freedom to be disrespectful to your rules and household. This can become a very challenging time especially if you have younger children at home who may be influenced by their older sibling.

If they do not want to respect you as the parent and head of your household, you may need to invoke your parental power to expel them from your household in order for them to truly experience what it is like living as an adult.

This may be a very difficult decision to make, but may be warranted if your adult child is disrupting your home and negatively influencing their younger siblings.

Following, some single moms share their parenting strategies that have helped them reclaim and maintain their parent power!

"We must establish household rules and consequences and follow through when our children get out of line. We should strive to live the values we teach our children instead of just lecturing. Be the parent; put in the time to nurture, balance and love with discipline. Don't discipline in anger. Let them know you care."

Julie H. Dennis, New Jersey

"I treat my children's father with a good deal of respect and there is no drama between us. I respect him as the father of my kids and they know that. Secondly, I treat my children's feelings with respect and give them space to talk about their feelings. In our house, we have solid routines and a lot of discipline, which was missing from my life when I was married. It took a lot of hard work to get the routines in place, and I feel it has paid off. The kids know they can count on dinner together every night, breakfast together every morning, and 30 minutes of story-time with me. My house is a place of comfort and retreat and they always enjoy being here. That is something I am most proud of."

Kelley Nayo, California

"Be a great communicator with your children. Be honest with them; enjoy them; love them; bring them joy; allow them to make choices and know that you support them, and have boundaries because your children must obey you - understand that they are not your best friends, that you cannot say anything to or share everything with them."

Laticia Bailey, New Jersey

"I'm still learning how to parent, as my child is only nine and we have yet to experience the changes that come with the pre-teen and adolescent years. So far, I have been taking each experience and making the best possible decision I can. Life is about taking risks and learning from your mistakes and experiences. I approach parenting that way and try to teach my daughter to live by the same principle."

Monique Lawton, New Jersey

"A mother's love is divinely unconditional and cannot be compared to anything else. I know to always expect the unexpected or not to have expectations at all because people will disappoint you. I know for sure that I would not change one moment of being a mother with or without the struggle.
Because I love what I have been assigned to do, I do it with pride. I am not only a mother to my children but to others as well and I do not take it for granted."

Shanda Harris, New Jersey

PROJECT SINGLE MOMS CONTRIBUTORS

Chapter Five

SOMEONE IS ALWAYS WATCHING YOU

"The best way to make children good is
to make them happy."
Oscar Wilde

Sometimes it may be really hard to take a close look at our children because we may be afraid that we will see a mirror-image of ourselves. Our children tend to take on our physical characteristics as they develop into young adults. I often hear people say that my daughter and I look so much alike we could be twins. I will proudly admit that she does get most of her physical attributes from me. However, when she was much younger she resembled her father most.

There is very little we can do about how much our children resemble us physically. On the other hand, as parents we do possess some level of control over the type of person our children will develop into based on personality traits, behaviors and attitudes.

Oftentimes, it can be difficult for us to take an in-depth look into our mirrors for we may be afraid of what our hearts and minds may reveal about the women we have chosen to become as well as the single moms we have chosen to be to our children.

Whether or not we choose to accept it, we are the first role-models our children will interact with and take their cues from about making choices for their lives. The decisions we make for ourselves ultimately will directly and, in some cases, indirectly impact how our children, especially our daughters, will make decisions.

We must be especially careful about the choices we make regarding our finances and relationships. I am sure that many of us can attest that we have made poor choices in both areas of our lives and in many other areas. Our children are watching us and every decision (wrong or right) we make. They are listening to every word we speak about them, ourselves and about others. Their minds are soaking up, observing and processing our actions as the adult role-models in their lives. They are digesting the good, the bad and the ugly we exhibit to them.

Yes, we all make mistakes. However, what is most important is that when we make mistakes we learn from them and not repeat them especially in the presence of our children. It is also important that when we make mistakes, we take the time to explain to our children why we made the mistake, what we have learned from it, and that they should not make the same one.

We know that there are many external influences that our children look to as role-models. Between the media, celebrities, and Internet, our children are bombarded with all types of negative images and influences. Many children view celebrities as their role-models over their own parents.

Media and celebrities are very hard to compete with. However, if we start early to instill positive traits, characteristics, behaviors and attitudes into our children by serving as positive examples for them, we will have a better chance of raising healthy, productive and wise children who will not be easily influenced by these and other external influences.

We have the power to influence our children's actions and behaviors by serving as their first, official role-models.

Following, a few single moms share their perspectives on parents as role-models.

"Our children were not born with manuals. We are going to make mistakes, but we learn and grow from them."

Carla Alexander, New Jersey

"What I know now is to be strong, always hold my head up high and to never, ever put myself down. What you do and how you live will show up in your child."

Darlene Morgan, New York

"Teaching a boy how to be a man without a father-figure is tough for a woman. Instilling knowledge into my son, insight to life's turmoil, and helping my son learn what it means to earn a living is challenging. I do not always say the right things to my son and I do not always make the right decisions for him, but those flaws are minor compared to the person I have helped shape him into. My son is a wonderful, caring, empathic human being with a spirit and intelligence that would lift anyone up. We have struggled and we have overcome each obstacle with grace. I give myself ample credit for it."

Deborah Morillo, New York

"My greatest challenge as a single mom has been taking care of my daughter's health. It was also a challenge to fight the court system for custody of my son after he was removed due to domestic violence against me. I have been homeless for a long period of time but thanks to the grace of God I am in a transitional housing program and I'm going to have a stable home for my children. Also, I'm changing my life around to be a good example for my children."

Elsie Rivera, New Jersey

"Being able to provide for my children without being dependent on child support or government assistance is one of my greatest accomplishments as a single mom. The added benefit of this is that my kids can see that with God's help, hard work and determination does pay off. My goal is always to be a positive role-model for my children."

Faith McCalla, New Jersey

"My greatest accomplishments as a single mom are completing my doctorates degree in the midst of a divorce, recently completing the Governing Institute of New Jersey Leadership Program, and continuing to be a positive role-model for my two daughters."

Gayle Nelson, PhD, New Jersey

"I decided to start a business this year and it is taking off very nicely. My livelihood is a crochet business and I sell my products throughout Oakland. My kids see me earning money doing what I love and they are proud of my work. As my business grows, my confidence in my own skills and abilities are being restored and I love the way I feel each day. I feel like I can accomplish anything with hard work and diligence. My kids are learning that they too can do anything they want to do."

Kelley Nayo, California

"I am a single mother raising a daughter. It's very challenging because I have to be her role-model. I'm not with her biological father so it makes it even harder to raise her. I want to teach my daughter to be responsible and to be a go-getter. I want her to succeed in life. I want her to do all the things I didn't get to do because of having a baby in my early adult life.

I made it through high school and I waited six years to go to college. I thought to myself, 'How can I tell her to go to college when I didn't go myself?' So getting back in school was a plus for me even though it is hard. I'm pushing myself through and she is the reason why. I continue everyday so that I can provide a better life for her and show her this is the way it should be done."

Kemyyah Bohler, New Jersey

"My children know a lot about life but what I have instilled could never be enough because I'm only one person. Now when I think of something, I call a family meeting and pour it out, because I need them to be informed, to be on the track of living life and not just existing.

I don't want my children to fantasize that they don't need a father nor decide that their children can do without a father. I want them to have a life before a family and have a sound relationship with a faithful, compassionate, honest and respectful mate who will be a good father no matter what, before they dive into parenthood."

Laticia Bailey, New Jersey

"I'm ok with my ex-husband and being divorced, however, I am not ok with his approach or lack thereof to parenting. It's important that a child has both parents in their lives. Male and female role-models are very empowering to both sexes. An absent parent takes away from the child's well-being. It's almost like being under-nourished and it's not fair to the child at all. Although I really wanted a baby, I probably would have waited if I knew how challenging it would be to do it alone. I'm still trying to figure this out."

Lynnette Caldwell, New Jersey

"Getting my daughter's father to understand that the relationship he develops and nurtures with our girls will result in their future perceptions of men, and how they relate to men has been a great challenge as a single parent."

Nichole Harris, Maryland

"My greatest accomplishment as a single mom has been to be able to commit daily to live a life of virtue and integrity before my daughters."

Pamela Vail, New Jersey

"I would share with my daughter that in parenting, it is essential to make God a priority and never forget that children have a voice too. They have feelings and need to express them so it is good to just listen sometimes instead of turning them away or telling them to be quiet. Also, if you live life the way you teach life it makes it easier for you to be the example for them to follow and harder for them to try and not be like you. Lastly, do not cripple them by doing too much because they need to learn independence at home."

Shanda Harris, New Jersey

"I have four credits left to earn my Associates Degree. I see that my daughter is really proud of me when I get good grades and she tries even harder to do better with her grades. It's more like a friendly competition; she wants to do better than her mom. Once I'm done, I'll be going on for my bachelors, and my masters. I want to eventually be a counselor and motivational speaker for young girls and women. I've been focusing on why I'm here and what my purpose is on this earth. I know the trials and failures that have taken place in my life occurred so that I can share and be a blessing to someone else so that my failures become someone else's victories. So I've been focusing on serving and finding where there is a need.

My involvement with the youth ministry has definitely affected my daughter because she's more involved and she enjoys it and is opening up more on a spiritual level.

In 2006, I entered a beauty pageant for the first time in my life. At one time, I never thought that I would be considered beautiful to anyone. Once I allowed the Lord to really come in and show me my true worth, I mustered up enough courage to go and audition. I didn't leave with the crown, but I won 4th place, I received flowers, and trophies and it was an awesome experience. I've seen a huge change even in my daughter since I've started to do shows. She's become very proud of me, and has started to take more pride and attention in how she carries herself.

I have learned that my daughter needs to know my real trials and my issues. I explained to her how I got to be a single mother, and why we struggle the way we do at times. I don't want her to believe that everything is sweet all the time. I want her to understand and know that bad choices now at her age will affect the rest of her life. I'll still be in college finishing school when she goes to college. That's a blessing, but if I would've stayed on track I would've been finished by now."

Shanick Moore, New Jersey

"My greatest accomplishment as a single parent is being a role-model for my children. I was a pregnant teen and I knew that one day I would be faced with teenage girls that would possibly think having sex before marriage was okay because their mom did it. I had to accomplish some things in my life so that they could embrace the achievements that I made over the not-so-good decisions that I made. I graduated from high school. I attended college full-time, while working full-time to support them. I've held a position with the same company for 16 years. As they got older, I introduced them to as many cultural things as I could. I invested time in them as I matured. I am proud about that and consider it an achievement because it has contributed to the people they are today."

Simone Bellamy, New Jersey

"Providing for my kids and being a role-model for them has been a great challenge for me. However, being able to take care of my kids and still accomplish my Master's degree was a major accomplishment. I wish I knew that being a single mother would not be easy. I do my best and I realize that I am not perfect. I try to teach my kids that when they become parents they will have to love their kids and teach them the best values they can."

Susan Johnson, New York

"I know that I have to teach my children how to first let God lead their lives, get a financial planner, invest their money and work on the things that they desire after they have a well thought out plan for their futures."

Anonymous

"By becoming a published author, it shows my kids that they can accomplish anything they want! I am new to the arena as a single mom and am therefore still figuring it out as I go along. I have already learned that everyone needs someone and you can't be afraid to ask for help!

People constantly reinforce my parenting by stating that I am a good mother and to keep up the good work. If your mother-in-law and soon to be ex-husband states it, you are in good shape!"

TJ Dupree, New Jersey

"At age 21, I started dating a great guy. He accepted the fact that I had three young children and he treated all of us pretty nice. We were together for close to 7 years and on and off again for nearly 8 years afterwards. About a year ago, my youngest daughter questioned me about our relationship, asking if I thought that we would ever marry. I was shocked because the question really made me realize that she was watching me. I asked myself, 'How would I react to one of my daughters being involved with a man for more than 14 years that had not married her?' I knew as a mother, I would be upset. I felt like a hypocrite and it bothered me to think that my children may think that it was acceptable to me that my friend had not made a commitment to me. I ended my involvement with this person largely due to my daughter's discussion with me."

Anonymous

Chapter Six

SAY WHAT YOU MEAN AND MEAN WHAT YOU SAY

We shouldn't make idle threats to our children. Our word must be our bond because they know when we are just saying something just to say it. The first or second time they may think, "Okay, I better straighten up." But if it is the third, fourth, or fifth time and we are still making the same idle threats with no change in behavior from our children, we need to try a new strategy.

I hear some moms say to their child, "If you keep acting up I'm going to kick you out," or "If you keep acting up I'm going to call the police," or "If you keep acting up I'm going to send you to live with your Dad" but, they never go through with any course of action.

The only things we will accomplish with these idle threats are a further deterioration of our children's respect and trust in us. They will not respect or trust that we are going to follow through on what we are saying to them. So, what will they do? They will continue to act up and do things that they know we do not want them to do. After all, the only thing we are going to continue to do is make idle threats.

BE CONSISTENT WITH YOUR CHILD.

Sometimes as parents we want to have our cake and eat it too. It would be nice but I don't know how possible it is when it comes to raising teens. In other words, we expect perfect behavior but we sometimes fail to set clear boundaries. Before we start laying down the laws on curfews, dating, driving privileges, etc., we must be sure that we are in agreement with them and that we can live with and enforce the rules we have made for our children. We must be clear about the rules and willing to stick to what we tell them they can or cannot do. Once we begin to waver back and forth with the rules, we are setting ourselves up for unmet expectations and lots of walking outside the boundaries. When we are certain about and confident with the rules we have established, they should be communicated in such a manner that our children know we mean business and there will be serious consequences for them to face should they break the rules. In most cases, we can trust that they will follow the rules; unless we leave room to test them, which they normally do. Occasionally, it is alright to test us, but we should not waver unless they approached us in the correct manner.

When they approach us to request a change in the household laws or rules before they actually break the rules, we may want to take under consideration their request and even grant it for a special occasion or a one-time only event.

However, if they intentionally break the rules or laws and then proceed to act as though they somehow forgot the rules, they are testing us. Our children will continue to test us until we remind them of the serious consequences they will face if they break the rules again. Then, you should follow through with the appropriate discipline if it becomes necessary. We must be consistent and occasionally remind our children of the rules so they cannot use forgetting as an excuse. The more consistent we are with our children, the more consistent their behavior will be in abiding by our rules.

As parents, we must face the reality and realize that teens today are a different breed than those growing up in the years prior to 1980. If we want our children to behave a certain way and honor certain principles that we try to instill within them such as religious and cultural traditions, we must be consistent and not waver back and forth with our beliefs and morals.

Consistency is something I have worked hard to enforce with my daughter, especially during her pre-teen years. When we relocated to New Jersey in 1998, it was court-ordered that she would spend summers in Detroit with her father and we would alternate holidays. During the first five years of this summer routine, it was extremely challenging for me to not interfere with the parenting style of my ex-husband. He did not feel it was necessary to enforce some of the restrictions and rules I had established for my daughter.

It was evident that his parenting style was lax and resulted in an obvious shift in my daughter's behavior when she returned home from Detroit.

I had to re-program her by reminding her that certain behaviors and attitudes that may have been accepted in her father's household were not tolerated in mine. Fortunately, my daughter was able to adapt back to my expectations and, as she grew older, her behaviors and attitudes became consistent with my parenting style.

We have to be consistent, starting when our children are young, if we do not want them to question or doubt what we will approve, disapprove or tolerate.

Following, some single moms share their stories about the importance of consistent parenting with their children.

"My greatest challenge as a single mom is to not overindulge in my children's wants due to their father not being around. I found this especially hard with my daughter. Now I am in a situation that no matter what I do or give her it is not enough. This is because she craves her father's attention so much. However, she will never admit this. I have put her in counseling, but she no longer goes."

Elizabeth Lopez, New Jersey

"There have been a few challenges in my life, but the one that is on my heart now, is dealing with the fact that my ex-husband has moved in with a young lady and her child. It bothers me when I'm trying to raise my daughter in a certain way and to have certain morals. But when she visits her father for the weekends all the rules she has at home don't apply. I know I can't control what goes on in his home but, as the parents of our child, I feel that we both have an obligation to her. We must both be consistent parents and he should respect my wishes when she's with him. I feel that this simple thing can turn into something very big down the road. I guess I'm trying to say that it's hard to raise a child when one parent is going to church and trying to live according to the Word, and the other parent hasn't reached their season yet."

Natasha Taylor, New Jersey

Chapter Seven

TRY WALKING IN HER SHOES SOMETIMES!

"Don't limit a child to your own learning, for he was born in another time."
Rabindranath Tagore, Indian poet, playwright & essayist

When your daughter was younger, do you ever recall moments when she would dress up in your clothing, put on your makeup, and try to balance herself to keep from falling over while walking in your oversized shoes?

Sometimes as moms, we need to try walking in our daughter's shoes (figuratively) to better understand their perspectives on things we may have difficulty accepting.

Although it may be very challenging for us to do, we must remember that we were once teenage girls ourselves. We must face reality and acknowledge that things are different today. I am not saying that we should give our children all the freedom they desire. I am suggesting that we become more open-minded and allow ourselves to reflect back on how things were when we were growing up and how we were raised by our parents.

I often reflect on my teenage years. When I was growing up, my mother was extremely strict with me. At least, that is how I felt. She was very closed-minded about allowing me to date and talk to boys on the phone. I did not go on my first real date until after I graduated from high school. Really! Now that I am grown, I will admit some things to you, but do not tell my mother. She still does not know these things. I did sneak behind her back to talk on the phone to my high school sweetheart and even went on some dates during my latter high school years. It really was not my fault. I am going to blame my oldest sister should my mother read this book and my secrets are revealed. You need to know that I am the baby of the family; lucky number 13. To my mom, I am her 40 something year-old baby daughter.

It was my sister who extended me courtesies to date and enjoy my teenage years. My sister knew how strict my mom was and that my mom was from the old school of parenting. (There is a generational gap since my mom gave birth to me when she was 42). My sister came to my rescue and allowed me to enjoy a little freedom and fun during my teen years. My mom was not open-minded at all and therefore, would never attempt to walk in my shoes. If anything, if I ever got out of line, she would knock me out of my shoes. Remember, she is an old school parent.

I used to wonder why my mom was so strict on me. After all, I was an excellent student in school, went to church every Sunday willingly, and was a well-mannered child. I would think to myself, how could she be so tough on me; especially since she married at the young age of 16? When I was 16, all I wanted to do was date one boy and talk on the phone. I wasn't thinking about getting married at such a young age. So, why couldn't my mom understand that I just wanted to be a teenage girl and do what other teenage girls were doing? There were many times I wanted my mom to walk in my shoes so that she could better understand me and know that she could trust me.

As I became an adult, I began to understand the choices and decisions my mother made while raising me. I realized that I am the person I am today because of the choices my mother made and that her actions were intended to protect and not to hurt me. I am grateful to my mother for wanting to shield me from choices she may have made when she was younger and that she did not want me to repeat her mistakes. I now realize that she probably held on so tightly to me because I was her youngest child and she did not want me to make the same mistakes as some of my older siblings.

Nevertheless, at the age of 16, I made a vow that when I had a daughter, I would not be as strict as my mother. I did not want my daughter to feel that she had to lie to me or sneak behind my back to do anything.

Therefore, we should try to imagine ourselves walking in our daughter's shoes and ask ourselves, "If this was me, how would I respond to my mother?" The reality is sometimes we do not want to admit that we would probably respond to our mothers the same way our daughters respond to us. Today, parenting does require you to be more open-minded and willing to make some compromises.

"Remember that whatever you sow into them is what you will reap from them. Talk to your children about your upbringing and allow them to be who they are. Help them to discover what they excel in and encourage them always to do their best. Our children are watching how we behave towards other people and when placed in certain situations, monitor your own actions."

Charisse Roberts, New Jersey

"It is a challenge knowing when to let go and give my children autonomy to make certain decisions. At times it seems that my mind has not fully grasped that they are older and competent in some areas. I guess the good news is that I am aware of this discrepancy so I consciously question certain decisions and run it by friends to get a second opinion."

Faith McCalla, New Jersey

"Little girls will grow to be women someday and they need to know the difference between being loved and being used and thinking it's love. That's why I have a hard time with raising my little girl. There is a fear in my mind that because her biological father is not in her life she will turn to the wrong man looking for love or turn to a drug looking for that fullness that she didn't get from her father because she thinks that she's not good enough to be wanted by him."

Kemyyah Bohler, New Jersey

"Another challenge is parenting a teenager. Times are different in that children are being killed in record numbers these days. It's difficult to convey to my daughter that I trust her but I don't trust others. Parents aren't even as responsible as they should be and therefore, their children aren't where they should be mentally. I continually express that I understand her desire to have fun and frequent certain places but caution and responsibility take precedent over all else. Therefore, she becomes defiant and causes a bitter situation. However, as I continue to speak with her, she appears to understand what I'm talking about. Most parents make the mistake of befriending their children. That'll never work. When my daughter becomes a parent, I would advise her not to be too strict or too lenient but to find a perfect balance. Being overbearing causes children to be sneaky and being too lenient causes them to hook up with the wrong crowd. When in doubt, consult your spirit because your spirit will always direct you in making the right decision."

Lynnette Caldwell, New Jersey

"Due to the age of my children, I try to make information relevant to their current situation so that there is a stronger connection. It is also important to establish a network of women from different ages and backgrounds to serve as your sister parents. Put your egos aside and really watch how your young ladies blossom when allowed the freedom to love and make choices."

Makeda Hunter, New Jersey

"I am tired a lot and I lose my patience and start yelling more than I want to. My daughter will be a teenager tomorrow and that teenage-female-attitude is enough to drive even the most patient person insane. My daughter is great though because she knows me, and when I am just cranky and being ridiculous, she will nicely tell me I need to take a nap. That is her signal for 'Mom, can you hear what you are saying!'

Parenting requires incredible patience. You have to be open and willing to listen, even when you do not agree. Parenting is not about always being right but acknowledging the fact that you do not have all the answers."

Miriam Parrotto, New Jersey

Chapter Eight

BE INFORMED AND AWARE OF TEEN CULTURE

If you are not, you should become aware of what teens are talking about and the language they use especially when text messaging. For example, did you know that OMG is "Oh My God" in teen talk?

As parents, we should investigate and be in tuned to the activities in which our children are involved. For instance, do you know whether or not your daughter has a MySpace or Facebook page? Have you seen her page? If you answered no, get busy and find out. I make impromptu visits to my daughter's MySpace and Facebook pages every other month. I have made her remove pictures and text that misrepresents who she is and may send the wrong message to the wrong person. Again, it is about proactive parenting.

We need to research and check out some of the popular teen websites such as Gurl.com which is pretty safe and www.sexetc.org and see what teens are talking about. It is amazing that our children are not shy or afraid to express their feelings and show their true selves online. They are not shy about discussing their thoughts and feelings about sex or drugs.

We, as parents, should become informed about the illegal drugs available to them in their schools and our communities; as well as the medications in our medicine cabinets which some teens use in order to experience a high.

Learning about how our teens spend their time when they are not with us and/or are behind closed doors in their bedrooms must be a priority for the proactive parent. We must always try to be aware of attitude and behavior changes in our children and be prepared to take action to address their attitudes and behaviors. When we are more informed about teen culture, we will be better equipped to respond proactively should we need to seek help. Let's stop living in the dark ages and become "New Age" parents who can keep up with today's teenagers. Our children already think we do not understand them or anything about teen culture. Unfortunately, this is true in many cases with some parents who choose to ignore that times are different.

Our children were not born with instruction manuals and, in many cases, we just do not have a clue about how they think, especially during their teen years. Sure, maybe you have already raised one teenager and managed to live to talk about it, but I am certain you can attest that although they may fall from the same tree, they are a different apple every time.

"My mother raised me to be able to come to her and communicate with her openly and honestly with regards to any subject matter; sex, drugs, etc. I pride myself that in this day and age I am raising my daughter the same way. She is being raised "old school" with a firm disciplinarian (not necessary by spanking). She is raised with a firm hand to know that she is the child and I am the adult. She is my best friend as well and she knows that we can talk about anything."

Carla Alexander, New Jersey

"My greatest challenges as a single mom have been trying to get my daughter to believe in the importance of education, the importance of setting goals and not being influenced by peer pressure. The challenge comes into effect when her so-called friends try to influence her to smoke, have sex or do things that she knows are incorrect. With television, music and the low self-esteem that exists in today's young girls, they are left with a lot of pressured choices. I always tell my daughter to ask any 10 single mothers what is the most important thing they wished they had done before becoming a mother and I would bet that 8 out of 10 would say to get a better education."

Cassandra White Graves, Ohio

"My daughter tells me constantly that I am the best mom in the world, she is so happy that she has a smart mom who works very hard and teaches her a lot of things. She likes the fact that I am still young and 'hip' compared to some of her friends' parents. She also admires me for continuing to go to college and work full-time to be a good role-model for her. She feels that she can come to me and talk to me about anything and everything (as she does)."

Danielle Felder, California

PROJECT SINGLE MOMS CONTRIBUTORS

Chapter Nine

CREATE A SUPPORT SYSTEM THAT WORKS

As single moms it can be extremely difficult managing all of the responsibilities that we tend to undertake. It becomes increasingly more difficult when we try to do it all by ourselves. It is essential that we put a support system in place. It will save us all some gray hairs and help our lives become a little more manageable.

When I relocated to New Jersey in 1998 with my daughter, then 8-years-old, I left behind all my family in Detroit. We did not know anyone and had no relatives in New Jersey. My job required me to work 12 hours most days, which included evenings and weekend hours.

I panicked for a moment because I needed someone to care for my daughter when I had to work evenings and could not bring her to work with me. I shared my dilemma with some of my co-workers and instantly they were recommending family members and in the end it all worked out.

Of course, I did learn everything about my daughter's caregivers before I agreed to leave her in their care. I was hesitant to ask for help initially, but after I did, I had other co-workers offer to care for my daughter when they were not working. I met female friends at my church and they became my daughter's co-moms and Aunties. Either way, they were happy to assist me and even offered to baby-sit when I did not need it so that I could have some time for myself. Do not be afraid to ask for help. We all need it!

TAKE AND MAKE TIME FOR YOURSELF.

After all is said and done, if you do not make time to take time for yourself, you run the risk of mental and physical burn-out. When you are sick, you are no good to anyone. You may feel like to you cannot take time off from work because no one knows how to do your job and you are too valuable an employee to go on vacation or take a sick day.

Let me enlighten you. Believe me when I say you are replaceable and there is always someone willing to do your job for less pay.

Although you may be loyal to your employer, their loyalty is to the company and to make sure that the work gets done with or without you.

You must regularly schedule "ME" time away from everything and everybody, especially the kids. It is much better that they live without you for an hour, day or weekend, than to live without you for a lifetime.

"My greatest challenge as a single mom has been never finding any "ME" time. Because I don't drive, it has also been a great challenge trying to get to and from various locations. I have three beautiful, smart daughters that love me unconditionally. Upon raising them, I wanted more than anything in the world for them to love me, respect me and admire me for my hard work and dedication. I wanted them to grow up knowing that I have been the very best mother I could be. I wish I knew before that it was 'OK' to accept help and that I didn't have to be afraid to ask for help. I needed to stop thinking that I could be "SUPER MOM," because I burnt myself out."

Acquanetta King - New Jersey

"What I know for sure today as a single mom is that a child needs both a male and female in their lives. I don't like to hear single moms say "I or my children don't need anyone in our lives!" I believe that statement is so far from the truth."

Cassandra White Graves, Ohio

"I know it is difficult to raise a child as a single parent. That is why you must surround yourself with positive people and you will find they will not only uplift your spirit, but will support you in many areas of your life. This way you do not feel alone!"

Charisse Roberts, New Jersey

"Asking for help is okay and not a sign of incompetence or weakness. I also wish I knew that it was okay to put myself first at times. I learned the hard way that doing this was not a sign of weakness but a sign of strength. It is necessary for my overall wellness. To know that it was okay to say "no" and I don't have to be everything to everyone was invaluable. I learned that this is a healthy way to set boundaries."

Faith McCalla, New Jersey

"Balancing career with parental responsibilities has been a major challenge for me in parenting. In addition, I needed to learn to ask for help and make trade-offs to make my support network effective."

Julie H. Dennis, New Jersey

"Getting used to the idea of being single, not having dependable help, and financial ups and downs are some of my greatest challenges as a single mother. I spend a lot of time with my children and sacrificed a corporate career in favor of being able to spend time with the kids. As a result of those choices, I don't have much money and it is still challenging getting used to that concept. I don't have a community of my own yet with people I can call for assistance or count on. I often feel very alone in this child-raising effort, which is not a comfortable feeling."

Kelley Nayo, California

"Support is the key ingredient and provides a buffer from both experienced and impending distress! For me, it definitely helped to stay in prayer and better my relationship with God. My family provided additional emotional, physical, and financial support. My advice to others is to seek support in all forms whether from family, friends, partners, God, Allah, etc."

Nichole Harris, Maryland

"I wish I was aware prior to being a single mother of how the teenage years were some of the toughest to get through. But with the help of a village, I am able to raise productive children."

Pamela Vail, New Jersey

"I am still learning. Being a single mom does not mean that you need to prove to anyone that you are "superwoman." Although I was very hesitant to ask for help with my daughters at certain times, there were times that I should have asked for more help instead of having the "stress" of doing "everything" on my own. Single moms need lots of support, and I found out quickly that if you don't ask, it is rarely offered. I also found out that the people that understood what I was going through the most were other single moms."

Robyn Lynn Blocker, New Jersey

PROJECT SINGLE MOMS CONTRIBUTORS

Chapter Ten

ASSESS THE QUANTITY AND QUALITY OF TIME YOU SPEND WITH YOUR CHILD

"Your children need your presence more than your presents."
Jesse Jackson

ROI (Return on Investment) is a term used in business transactions. The premise is when an investor is considering putting up money to support a venture, they want to know what their ROI will be or how much money they stand to make over a specified term; the point, they hope, at which their investment should begin to yield results or profits.

The term ROI is also very relevant when it comes to parenting. In this case, think of our children as the venture (or in many cases adventure).

You, as the parent, are the investor. An investor's goal is to always turn a profit or reap great rewards for their investment. The same applies to our children. The more we invest our time and attention into our children, the greater the reward or the return on our investment.

You may be thinking that there are great risks with investing. This is true. However, let me assure you the risks are much greater when we choose not to invest our time and attention into our children. I assure you that the more time and attention invested in your child will yield great dividends in the long-term. What will your ROI be?

Now, we will talk about quantity versus quality which are also terms used in businesses such as manufacturing and research. These terms can also be applicable to assessing the amount of time and the value of the time we choose to spend or invest in our children.

Quantity refers to the amount of time we spend with our child(ren). Most single moms tend to lead very busy lifestyles and not always by choice. Our lifestyles which often include work, church, relationships, hobbies, etc. may prohibit us from spending as much time with our children as we desire.

Let's take a moment to assess our time. There are 24 hours in a day. The average work day is usually 8 hours. However, for single moms, our average work day can range from 8 -12 hours a day considering over-time and the second job. Now, factor in the other things that you allocate time to do daily such as your commute to/from work; church activities; volunteer activities; and school. Do not forget the time you allocate to a relationship with the opposite sex should you be so fortunate to have one.

Most of our days begin at 5 or 6am and end at 10 or 11pm after you have cooked dinner; washed dishes; put the younger kids to bed; and prepared for the next work day.

What about sleep? They say that we should average 8 hours of sleep each night. Is this truly possible for single moms? Well, let's consider this for those single moms who are able to get 7-8 hours of sleep in each night.

Now, do your own calculation to determine exactly how much time you actually spend with your child(ren) each day. If you do not work, this calculation may not be applicable to you.

However, if you do fall into the category of the single mom who does work, go to church, volunteer, go to school and have a relationship with the opposite sex, you are lucky if you calculate spending 3-4 hours daily with your child(ren).

So, if you only average 3-4 hours each day with your child(ren), what is the quality of this time?

Perhaps your 3-4 hours is during meal-time. Do you eat dinner together as a family or do you grab your plates and each person heads to their separate rooms to eat dinner?

Perhaps your 3-4 hours is during drive-time when transporting your child to/from school or their sports activities. Do you spend your drive time discussing what is happening in school or learning about your child's new friends, or is the car radio blasting and your child(ren) tuned into music on their own iPods?

Five years ago, I chose to slow my life down for a moment to access and measure the quality and quantity of the time I was spending with my daughter Daphne.

It was one evening in 2002 that revealed that I was not yielding the best Return on Investment as a single parent. My 12-year-old daughter approached me in the kitchen as I was preparing dinner and said to me, "Mom I know you love me, but do you like me?" As I pondered the sincerity of her question that evening, I realized that although I had been investing a lot of effort to provide for her physical needs, I had been falling short with my investment in her emotional needs.

I also knew that if I did not make time to let her know that she was my number one priority, she would eventually begin to seek time and attention from other unhealthy and unwise sources such as the internet, boys and her peers.

Over the past five years, I have had to work hard to increase my Return on Investment and to substantially enhance the quality and quantity of time I spend with my daughter so that she never has to question whether or not she is loved and liked by me.

I am not suggesting that we equate our children to business transactions. However, I am suggesting that, from time to time, we may want to use these business applications to measure our effectiveness as parents by the quantity and quality of our time spent with our children. This approach has definitely helped to strengthen the relationship between my daughter and me.

Below, write a snapshot of how you may spend a typical 24-hour day by noting the activities that consume your day. Be sure to write in the time periods you spend with your child(ren). For time periods allocated to your child(ren), write down what occurs during this time.

6:00 a.m. _____

7:00 _____

8:00 _____

9:00 _____

10:00 _____

11:00 _____

12:00 p.m. _____

1:00 _____

2:00 _____

3:00 _____

4:00 _____

5:00 _____

6:00 _____

7:00 _____

8:00 _____

9:00 _____

10:00 _____

11:00 _____

12:00 a.m. _____

1:00 _____

2:00 _____

3:00 _____

4:00 _____

5:00 _____

"My greatest challenge as a single mom has been having extra time to enjoy fun things with my daughter. I try to do what I can to make my daughter happy but sometimes it is hard. I do not have a lot of free time to spend with her, and there really is no extra money for going out, but I do what I can to make things fun."

Amy Carlton, Pennsylvania

"The love I receive from my four children and thirteen grandchildren is the greatest benefit from being a single mom. I wish I knew when I first became a mother how precious spending quality time with family can be. I know for sure today that it is imperative to treasure special moments with our children. There were too many hours I worked to provide material things at the expense of moments with my children."

Brenda Jenkins, Michigan

"All of my sacrifices for my daughter have thus far been well worth it. As a single mom who is constantly budgeting- when it comes to my daughter's needs - I have always found a way."

Carla Alexander, New Jersey

"Savor those moments while they are little and dependent on you. Be in the moment and appreciate the special times you have together. Children grow up way too fast and you can never go back and recapture those moments in time."

Christina Rowe, Florida

"Relax and enjoy parenthood. Once you realize that it is a blessing to raise kids, you can relax into the knowledge that you are doing what you have been put here to do. Let go of the notion that being alone is a burden because if you feel that way, you will miss all the fun stuff. Do things with your kids so that they will have fond memories of their childhood with you, rather than scar tissue. Find at least one or two good friends who you can call when you think your head is about to explode."

Kelley Nayo, California

"I've had to work extremely hard to make a decent living for my family and yet I don't get to spend as much "quality" time with my children as I would like to. Since I'm in work mode most of the time, I don't get a chance to do some of the "creative" things or more tedious things that my children request."

Robyn Lynn Blocker, New Jersey

PROJECT SINGLE MOMS CONTRIBUTORS

Chapter Eleven

CANDID CONVERSATIONS WITH WOMEN ON HOW THEY BECAME SINGLE MOMS

"A divorce is like an amputation: you survive it,
but there's less of you."
Margaret Atwood, Canadian Writer

MY STORY:

After three long years of dealing with verbal abuse and just being plain unhappy to the point of where it affected both my attitude and my appearance, I finally found the strength within me to walk away. I was married at the tender young age of 22. He was in the Marine Corps when we met through my niece and her husband. It was love at first sight, I thought. After a family tragedy which brought us closer, we became engaged four months after meeting. A year later, his service with the Marine Corps ended and we married against the wishes of my mother and family. They all thought I was too young to marry and felt I would not complete my college education if I did.

Well, of course, I did not listen. I proceeded with my wedding plans without my mother's blessing. She eventually came around toward my wedding date because she was now convinced that I was going to do it, with or without her blessing. As the story goes, I should have listened to my mother. But then again, I would not have had my beautiful daughter Daphne, so I am grateful for the experience which blessed me with my child and the strength I gained as a result of it. A week after we were married, I recall thinking to myself, "this is not going to work." I realized that I was not in love with this man, but infatuation led me to believe differently. No one ever teaches us the difference between love and infatuation. That is another book by itself. My foresight proved correct. For the next 2-1/2 years, I endured my ex-husband's verbal abuse, insults and selfish ways to the point that I stopped caring about myself. We separated twice and reconciled under false pretenses. I stayed as long as I did because of the vows I made before God: through the good and the bad and because I wanted my baby daughter to have two parents in her life. On July 4th, 1991 during a barbeque over my sister's house, I was lying across my sister's bed staring out the window. My eldest sister walked in and sat on the bed beside me. She said, "Steph, I'm not trying to get into your business, but the family is worried about you. You're not the same Stephanie we all know and love. Take it from me, after being in two physically abusive marriages, it's not worth it! You can be unhappy by yourself."

I did not even respond to her, but I knew she was right. That evening at home alone with my daughter, I called my sister crying uncontrollably and said, "I'm ready to leave." She said with much relief, "Okay, it's going to be alright. Let me make some calls and we (my brothers) will come and pack you and Daphne up to leave when he leaves for work in the morning." This was so there would not be any confrontation between my ex-husband and my brothers. Leaving my marriage was not an easy decision to make but one I knew I had to make for my daughter's sake. The months following were hard, and although he asked me to come back, I knew I could not. It took me over a year to finally become at peace with my decision and to know that God was not angry with me for breaking my vows and leaving my marriage. I had to believe that it was not His will for me to remain in an unhealthy and unhappy marriage. I never looked back and I am so glad I stood firm on my decision.

We become single moms for different reasons such as infidelity, domestic violence, abandonment for other women (usually younger ones), pre-marital pregnancy, or simply through our own fault.

In this chapter, single moms share their stories about how they were introduced to single motherhood.

HER STORY:

"It was during the 10th year of marriage when I realized I wanted out; we had simply grown apart. What was once fun when we were in our 30s, no longer held any value for me. I looked at my partner for life and could not see myself growing old with him. Habits that I thought he would leave behind such as partying and "smoking trees" seem to follow him for a whole decade. That was not what I wanted for our children. I wished for the days of lounging in the park enjoying a picnic or taking the kids for a stroll through the zoo - his response was always he was either too tired or did not have the money for such frivolous things.

After the first of two marriage counseling sessions over the course of two years, lies and deceit, and infidelity, I accepted the fact that we were headed in two different directions and neither of us were happy. I prayed for guidance and strength to do what was right and finally I prayed for God to take the fear of change away from me. It has been a year and some months since he has left our home and through the grace of God, the children and I are making it.

The mortgage is being paid, the children are in the same amount of activities as when they were the product of a two-parent home and I am really at peace."

HER STORY:

"I'd lived a sheltered life, had really low self-esteem and wasn't the greatest communicator. Boyfriends and relationships were not introduced to me by experience. I learned about relationships and communicating by reading (probably the wrong books) and also pining to have what I thought I saw others my age experience (boyfriends in high school, proms). I was shy and insecure, and had spent my adolescent years all the way up to 10th grade being teased about my looks.

My relationship grew closer with the young man in my life - spending time together, going to concerts, and having sex when spending nights at his or my apartment. I didn't know enough about myself...who I was or was not and had not begun to grow in self-love. We used birth control, or I did - the pill and when one made me ill my physician switched me to another -- and I didn't do the best job of using the new one.

I had to tell my male friend I was pregnant and he immediately began to put a plan in action for me by finding out where I could get an abortion.

At age 19, I had never thought about being pregnant, whether I'd have children, marriage or any of the responsibilities that I've come to learn are monumental when it comes to parenting. I became angry about his choosing for me and then even humiliated when my boyfriend told me that he felt sorry for me because I hadn't lived and I was going to miss out on life. He was right. Deciding to become a single mom has been a great sacrifice. I'd never thought about being pregnant and I'd never thought about having an abortion.

There were so many things I didn't think about, I just became a person who was in a situation and I began to do the things that the situation required - preparing to be pregnant and having a baby. My boyfriend went through denial and anger about me not agreeing to abortion, and played around with other women.

Our relationship spiraled to an end as I refused to allow him back into my life after months of pregnancy were spent without him. We were both young and not ready for the great challenge that was conceived in our young love. I subsequently moved on after our son was a year old and moved away a year later."

HER STORY:

"I became a single mom unwillingly. I was always taught to protect myself if I wanted to engage in sex. I can honestly say I have tried to protect myself to the fullest. While having sex with my daughter's father, he became upset because I told him I didn't want him to father any of my children if I decided to have any. I always used my own condoms but just this one day I decided I wanted to have sex but I didn't have a condom so he had one and I decided it was okay to use his condom. I was not aware I was pregnant until my cousin told me I was sleeping too much. I was also working at the time so I thought I was extra tired from working. I went to the doctor that following week and they told me I was 8 weeks pregnant. I thought I was going to pass out. I was angry because I knew I used a condom and it didn't break. When I told my boyfriend he didn't seem to be surprised. He later told me out of anger that he impregnated me on purpose. When I met him he already had two children, a boy and girl. My daughter's father is 10 years older than me. I thought he would be around because he was a good provider for his other children but I was wrong. I went through the entire pregnancy by myself. I moved into my own apartment when I was three months pregnant. I had no furniture in my house. I was sleeping on an air mattress on the floor. I was sick for the first six months of my pregnancy and I worked nights to pay my rent. I was a fool for him and let him come to my house anytime. When I was admitted into the hospital I called him and he said he was on his way. He never showed up before or after I had my daughter. When I sent him a picture of our daughter from my camera phone, his mom didn't think the baby resembled their family. I was very hurt. Yet, I still allowed him to walk in and out of my life. I finally became fed up and I knew I had a child to raise on my own. I wanted to put all my love into my daughter. It's now a whole year and a half later and he hasn't seen my child since she was 3 months old. I send pictures to him because he is now incarcerated just so he can see what he is missing out on. I now have a new man in my life who loves my daughter as his own and is a great father figure."

HER STORY:

"My marriage was dissolved after experiencing very limited food to feed my children and getting behind in bills. My husband was addicted to drugs and had little success with kicking the habit after numerous attempts to get clean. My emotional state was bad and I perceived life as no hope. After getting counseling, more education and a job, I was able to see hope. Unfortunately my husband's condition did not improve and I chose to end the marriage."

HER STORY:

"My ex-husband was a burnt-out Vietnam veteran who also had issues with his mental health that eventually caused us to separate. He too was unable or unwilling to be there for our children which was sad for my kids. When I realized I was alone, I decided to accept it after some time and talks with God. I then became willing to take on any and every battle I had to face. My son had a learning disorder but I pushed him to continue his education no matter how hard or long it took. My daughter developed mental problems and obesity but I still pushed her towards artistic outlets and embraced her bipolar health issues.

I walked through my mother's bouts with cancer, open heart surgery, mental breakdowns, and multiple sclerosis that rendered her crippled. I was determined to still have a life including travel and broadening of our life experiences. I buried my father and my sister when my husband walked away from our marriage."

HER STORY:

"I remember staring at a mountain of unpaid bills, quietly asking myself, how did I get here? Months before, I led what looked like an idyllic life. Married for 13 years with four wonderful children, I felt secure. We owned a beautiful six bedroom home in the New Jersey Suburbs. I worked part-time running our business, a hair and nail salon, while my husband had a good job as a network analyst at a large company. We went on vacations, remodeled our home and seemed to have it all. Then one day, after the salon had closed, an employee nervously pulled me aside. I could tell by the look on her face that something was bothering her. "It's your husband," she said. "There's something you should know." Time seemed to stand still as she told me about the rumors she had heard. Apparently my husband was having an affair with one of our employees.

I confronted my husband and he denied it. But the evidence quickly began to mount against him. He was not acting like himself. He would pick fights with me and then stay out all night. Things grew increasingly tenser by the day.

Then one bright, warm October day my world fell apart. During an argument, my husband twisted my arm and threatened my life. My marriage was over. What followed can only be described as a living hell. There was a restraining order issued. My husband moved out of the house and two weeks later, his girlfriend moved in with him."

HER STORY:

"I became a single mother my junior year in college. The truth about how and why that occurred is a story I will never share with my daughter, but no matter the reason, it was definitely the right decision. As a full-time student, raising my daughter alone meant sleeping 4-5 hours, studying until midnight, and leaving the house at 7 a.m. to take my daughter to day care on a bus in another town and getting to campus in time for my first class. Looking back, I have no idea how I survived those years, but in my heart I knew we would not make it if I did not finish my degree. Still, I became a welfare mother living off scarce benefits and student loans that covered the rent. It was tough and after finishing my degree in 1997 and completing my first year in law school, I was $96,000 in debt in student loans. The strain of graduate school with a very young child proved to be too much and during my second year in law school, I withdrew and found a job. I simply could not afford to live while in school and I had to make a very difficult decision."

HER STORY:

"I was married for 12 years to a guy I met while in college. Our marriage was without incident - we followed the recipe for middle class success. We both got master's degrees a couple of years after we finished college. We worked in corporate America and moved around the country trying to climb the corporate ladder. We bought a brand new tract house in the suburbs of a big city, and had kids. I found that the weight of being bread winner and primary caregiver for everybody was too much. When I expressed my concerns to my husband at the time, the differences in our values started to cause lots of conflicts. I believe that having children changes women in dramatic ways in a short period of time, beginning from the day you find out you are pregnant. The effect on the fathers is very different and far more gradual. For the most part, they are spectators while the women are active participants immediately upon inception. For me, becoming pregnant changed the way I view the world and I no longer look to material things for the pursuit of happiness. I wanted to use my energy toward enjoying my kids and the rest of my life as well. The way I saw it, our children were a blessing. To my ex-husband, the children became a barrier to his constant pursuit of wealth. When your family values are that different, you will always have discord between you."

HER STORY:

"I became a single mom by choice. I have always known that I would never get married. I did know that I wanted to educate myself and to have only one child, specifically a daughter. The man that I chose to be the father of my daughter happened to be a man that I respected and was great friends with prior to entering into an intimate relationship. I discussed with him at the start of the relationship that I was thirty years old and ready to have a child and if he wanted to enter into a relationship with me; I felt he needed to know where I was at in my life and what I needed."

Chapter Twelve

SOMETIMES OUR FLESH GETS WEAK

CANDID CONVERSATIONS WITH SINGLE MOMS ABOUT SEX

"Food has replaced sex in my life,
now I can't even get into my own pants."
Anonymous

MY PERSPECTIVE:

Boy, this is a very touchy subject and, at times controversial; especially if you practice a religion that dishonors those who engage in sex outside of marriage.

I will be the first to admit that I have fallen off the wagon occasionally as a Christian woman. Please do not judge me or any of our single moms who are brave enough to speak candidly about sex as a single woman; and a single mother. Here is something for you to remember while reading these stories including mine: "Judge not, lest ye be judged", Matthew 7:1.

I will say that the few times (no numbers necessary) I gave in to the flesh, I did truly repent my actions. I now practice celibacy and I thank God for moving me to this place of contentment. I don't think about sex until I hear someone talking about it. My response is, "Oh, what is that?"

As a single mom, I have always separated my acts as a woman from my acts as a single mom. I have been mindful not to engage in any inappropriate acts in the presence of my daughter. I have never allowed a man, even when I had serious boyfriends move in with me or stay overnight with my daughter's knowledge.

Because we are women, we have physical needs and sometimes it is very challenging abstaining from desires to be touched, caressed, and very close intimacy with a man, especially a great smelling man. So, what are the rules for dating and having sex as a single mom? A few of our single moms give their candid perspectives on sex and the single mom.

"A woman's appetite is twice that of a man's; her sexual desire, four times; her intelligence, eight times"

Unknown

HER PERSPECTIVE:

"Sex as a Single Mom; hmmm. How do you go from getting hit off on the regular to lying in bed by yourself and having the hormonal level of a teenager in some serious heat? That is a challenge, especially when you are trying to live as a Christian on Sunday and keep your legs closed Monday through Saturday. Fortunately or unfortunately, a childhood friend reappeared into my life at the right time which made the transition in my marital status easier to bear. Conversation was easy, trust was built which made loving my friend a treasure. Keeping my love life separate from my mommy life is a trip - I feel like I lead two different lives.

By day, I am the fearless mom who is there for her kids. By night, I am a lonely woman waiting on my companion to give me an hour of his time so we can sit on the porch, hold hands and whisper dreams for the future at two o'clock in the morning. Needless-to-say, I am exhausted when I entertain the late night visits. Yes I repent, because whenever I get a chance (which is not often) to get some "relief" I take it and must always be prepared with protection tucked away in my makeup bag. Reaching my fourth decade of life and being single is no fun when I am at the height of my sexual peak!"

HER PERSPECTIVE:

"At this stage in my life it's about abstinence. However, in the past I have been in sexual relationships and spent time privately outside of my home away from the children or if I had company at home, my children were away. A year after I moved away with my son, I lived with a gentleman for years, so he was my sole partner and the only person my son (the only child at the time) saw in the home. I have to admit that wisdom was not what it is for me now. While I never exposed him to anything I believed was inappropriate, I would have done things differently where my children wouldn't meet or even be exposed by telephone, etc. to anyone.

First, I entered a relationship and allowed the man to live in my home with my children. After a while we got married because of the guilt I felt living in sin. Big mistake. Those few years were worst than all the years with my kids father (first husband). This relationship ended in divorce after he deserted me. (Praise God)

From that point on through prayer and learning God's word (actually living God's word) my desire for sex is not an issue. I now know that sex is reserved for the marriage bed and marriage should not be entered without knowledge and commitment by both partners."

HER PERSPECTIVE:

"I have had sex only two times in the 2-1/2 years I've been divorced, about one month after my separation. It felt so wonderful, yet so overwhelming and confusing that I haven't even dated since then. My children are demanding and my life outside of raising kids is also very demanding. Unlike I felt in my twenties, I no longer want sex for the sake of sex. I want that powerful and meaningful connection that turns sex into love making. It is difficult to find time for myself, let alone finding time to really connect with someone else. I have sex toys and spend quality time with them several times a week. Not a day goes by that I don't wake up wishing I had someone to make love to, but I'm not willing to have sex without a solid relationship, and I'm not interested in starting a new relationship right now. I feel a new relationship would disrupt the very precarious balance I already have in my life. I hope that as my children grow older, I will have the energy to put into developing a serious adult relationship. In the meantime, it's me and the purple plastic penis."

HER PERSPECTIVE:

"I have always been a very open and liberated woman. I have developed the ability to distinguish love and sex; therefore in order to satisfy immediate needs, I do have friends with benefits. Sex now at the age of 44 is not as important to me as it was when I was in my 20's and 30's, especially now that I am raising a 14-year-old daughter that is built like a brick house. My daughter has only been introduced to a man that is of a committed and serious relationship. If it was up to her, I would not ever have sex again. But, she knows that will not be the case."

HER PERSPECTIVE:

"I deal with sex as a single mom by abstaining from having sex. Sex is one of the most important parts of being in a relationship with a man and at this time in my life, I haven't found a man who I want to share that part of my life with, so I abstain from sex. I could very easily go and approach any man for sex just for instant gratification, but that's not how I live my life. I am not looking for someone to live in the moment. I am looking for a partner for life, who is capable of being in a relationship through the good times and the hard times. A man will show you his genuine self, if first you become his friend and build on the relationship. With the spread of STD's and AIDS, I believe that it is important for me to spend time getting to know the man, his personality, his beliefs, his behaviors, and his actions. I must learn about his history and see the results of his AIDS test before I will enter into a relationship with him. My life is so important to me that I don't have time to waste on someone who does not have self-respect and love for self. I do look forward to some day having a loving marriage that involves lots of mutual respect, a clean bill of health, self-love, fun times and plenty of sex!"

Chapter Thirteen

REAL RAP FOR MY SINGLE TEEN MOMS AND TEEN TEMPTED: NOW WHAT?

Let me first begin by stating my disclaimer. I care deeply for all our teen daughters, especially those who have suffered from the lack of care, love and guidance from ineffective parents; which in some cases, has resulted in you becoming misguided and ill-equipped to make the wisest choice when it comes to premarital sex. My words are in no way meant to hurt, judge or offend our single teen moms. Those who know me, especially the teens I encounter regularly, are aware that Ms. Stephanie speaks from a place of truth and love, but she keeps it real.

TO MY SINGLE TEEN MOMS

Yes, you have made a choice that you will have to live with for the rest of your life, so you should know that the work has just begun raising your child. Parenting is a big responsibility you have decided to make in your young life. SO, NOW WHAT?

Through prayer, planning and preparation you can do it. You can take care of yourself and raise your child. It will not be easy, but it can be done. First, if you have not completed your education, JUST DO IT! You need it to ensure a decent future for yourself and your baby. DO NOT WAIT for others including your baby's daddy to take care of you. If he does not MAN UP, make him get up and step out of your life. GET UP AND MAKE IT HAPPEN FOR YOURSELF. You will respect yourself more when you challenge yourself to DO IT YOURSELF. Please do not rely on the system to raise your child. It should be temporary support to help you get on your feet. YOU ARE STRONGER THAN YOU THINK YOU ARE. You have someone depending on you. Your child did not ask to come here, but since you were so determined to bring her/him into this world, step up and HANDLE YOUR RESPONSIBILITY. There will be many times when you feel alone. YOU ARE NOT ALONE. There are resources to assist you but you must do some research to locate them. There are some resources listed at the end of this chapter. DON'T BE AFRAID OR ASHAMED TO ASK FOR HELP. READ and LEARN from the lessons learned and shared by the single moms in the previous chapters of this book who once walked in your shoes but MADE IT HAPPEN against the odds.

Do not let your decision to become a teenage mom define who you are. BE A SMART, DETERMINED YOUNG WOMAN who defines the kind of single mom she will become to her child (ren). It will not be easy, but live life, do not let life live you and become DEFEATED. LIVE THE LIFE YOU WANT! YOU CAN DO THIS! YOU MUST DO THIS for your sake and your child's.

Do not allow yourself to get caught up in the web of myths and labels society places on most single moms, especially teen mothers. KNOW YOUR WORTH and that YOU BRING VALUE to your child's life. YOU ARE NOT a baby-making machine. YOU DO NOT have multiple babies just for the paycheck. YOU DID NOT get pregnant just to have a man in your life. Just because your mother had you when she was a teenager does not mean you have to walk in her shoes, in this case. YOU CAN BREAK THE CYCLE!

ELIMINATE THE THOUGHT of having a baby because you need to feel loved and wanted. There are lots of people who love you and care about you, with plenty more to follow. YOU JUST DO NOT KNOW THEM YET, but they are closer than you think. And, SO WHAT if it feels better without a condom! You should know by now that when you have unprotected sex, you put yourself at risk of STDs, AIDS, HIV and other sexually transmitted diseases that may be lying dormant in your body.

HEAD UP! CHIN UP! CHEST OUT! Let's start the process of moving your life forward right now.

Now, go get a pen and start writing down your ACTION PLAN for your life. I want you to answer these questions and be specific. You can start taking notes here:

Question 1: What are your current needs? Separate your needs as a young woman from your needs as a teenage mom.

My needs for myself:

_____

_____

_____

_____

_____

_____

_____

_____

My needs as a Teenage Mom:

_____

_____

_____

_____

_____

_____

_____

_____

_____

Question 2:   What is your BIG picture?   Where do you see yourself in 5 years, 10 years?

In 5 years, I will be:

_____

_____

_____

_____

_____

In 10 years, I will be:

_____

_____

_____

_____

_____

Question 3: What are your personal goals? (i.e., I want to get my own apartment, I want to get my GED/High School Diploma)

My personal goals are:

_____

_____

_____

_____

_____

_____

_____

_____

Question 4: What are your professional goals? (e.g., I want to get a full-time job with benefits)

_____

_____

_____

_____

_____

_____

_____

Now, I want you to really think about the list of things you wrote that you need for yourself first, then as a teenage mom, and what your goals are. Do not be afraid to think BIG. If you believe it, you can achieve it!

When you are having a rough day and feel like you are dangling from a string, pull out your goals and read them and remind yourself that YOU ARE NOT DEFEATED! YOU CAN DO THIS!

I am going to challenge you to do something for yourself. Don't do it because I ask you to do it, do it because you know that you should in order to ensure a brighter future for yourself and your child.

I want you to mail, email or fax your needs and goals to me at my non-profit organization, My Daughter's Keeper. We will assist you in connecting with someone in your community to help you address your needs and work on achieving your goals.

My contact information is:

Stephanie Clark
My Daughter's Keeper, Inc.
1086 Livingston Avenue, Suite 2
North Brunswick, NJ 08902
P: (732) 565-9313 - F: (732) 565-1019

If you want to chat with me you can reach me on my MYSPACE page at www.myspace.com/msstephanie. If you are really serious about achieving your goals, and I truly hope you are, I expect to hear from you. IT IS NOT JUST ABOUT YOU ANYMORE.

TO MY TEMPTED TEENS WHO ARE HAVING PREMARITAL, UNPROTECTED SEX OR CONTEMPLATING HAVING SEX

Okay ladies, what do I, your parents, or society need to do to get you to keep your legs closed? Just keeping it real. You already know the risk you take when you engage in unprotected sex. Let's flip the script for a change. Instead of adults and research telling you what they think you want and need in order to get you to become more responsible and sensible teens about sex, how about YOU tell us! Seriously, I challenge every teen girl or boy who reads this book to reach out to me. Feel free to contact me through my MySpace page at www.myspace.com/msstephanie and let me know why you feel it is okay to engage in sex before marriage and why you so willingly put yourself at risk of getting pregnant?

I have met some of your mothers, so I know firsthand that many of you are not getting the proper guidance and information from home. Is this the deal? Again, it is not my intention to offend. Just keeping it real!

Perhaps your mother was a teenage mother and you feel that it is okay to follow in her footsteps and become a teenage mother too. PLEASE THINK AGAIN. You have the ability to stop the generational cycle of teenage mothers in your family. LET CHANGE BEGIN WITH YOU.

I know that today having sex is the popular thing to do to prove that you are part of the in-crowd. Ladies, what is up with this "wifey" thing? Believe me, you have time for that. I know it feels good when he tells you he loves you and calls you his "wifey" which I am told by my teenage daughter means that the guy is supposed to be really serious and committed to you even if you do not give him sex. If there is another definition for "wifey," email and educate me so I can educate other adults. Help me and the adults reading this book understand where we have failed you.

You may think you are ready and know what you are getting into when you get pregnant, but nine months later when the baby arrives and Bubba has decided to abandon ship, NOW WHAT? Do not just think about and get caught up in the moment. It is not only your life you put in jeopardy when you have unprotected sex. Your baby's future is in jeopardy as well, the moment he/she comes into the world; especially if you do not have a supportive parent or adult to help you raise your child.

I know that becoming a teenage mother in many cases happens unplanned and unexpectedly. In these cases if you choose not to become a single teen mom, DO NOT ABANDON

YOUR UNWANTED INFANT. Through the National Safe Haven program you can take your unwanted infant to your local hospital, police station or fire station WITH NO QUESTIONS ASKED. If you are not ready to take on the responsibility of being a single teen mom, there are hundreds of couples seeking and willing to adopt babies. YOU HAVE OPTIONS! Option #1 is to remain abstinent and have no sex at all until marriage. I know you have heard this before and sure you will do what you want to do but at least think seriously about your actions and their consequences before you act! Option #2 is to consider adoption if you know for sure that you are not prepared to care for and raise a child.

Hopefully you have read the chapters before this one and realize now that as a 30, 40 or 50 year-old single mom, Life as a Single Mom Isn't Easy and will most likely be even tougher as a single teen mom. What makes you think it will be easy for you? Love yourself, respect yourself and think about your future and how the decisions you make today will impact the rest of your life. Meet Lakeya Crone, our youngest single mom featured in this book.

HER STORY:

"Growing up and watching my mother struggle as a single parent of seven children, I would have never imagined that I would be in the same situation. I knew that getting pregnant at fourteen would be a challenge but I didn't know it was a struggle until I had to deal with day-to-day obstacles and still take care of my children with their fathers not by my side. Now being a single mother of two at the age of 19, I know I have much to learn but I know that I am capable of dealing with whatever life brings me.

My greatest challenges as a single teenage mom have been sacrificing my needs and putting my children first and also doing things for them that might not necessarily be the things that I want to do but it's so they don't have to struggle like I do. Also, trying to become financially stable and provide for my family without living paycheck to paycheck is a huge challenge. My greatest accomplishments as a single mom have been not letting anything stop me from reaching my goals and graduating from high school with two kids and now on my way to college. Another accomplishment for me is just being the best mom I can be and trying not to repeat the same mistakes as my mother.

Anyone can have a baby, but actually raising him or her is hard. What I know for sure today as a single mom is sometimes God calms the storm and sometimes he calms us in the midst of the storm and where there is no struggle there is no strength. I am stronger, wiser, more patient, and grateful. Although I am being the best mom I can be, I still think there is room for me to grow. The challenge is to grow and not stay in the same situation and learn from every experience. My advice to other single teen moms is that you have to pass by the thorns to get to the rose. It may not be what you planned for your life to be but you can break the cycle. Stay positive and believe that you do not go through things for no reason but it's to strengthen others and share your knowledge and wisdom from your experiences just as I am doing with you."

Below are some resources that I hope will be helpful to you.

MY DAUGHTER'S KEEPER, INC.: Provides mentoring, support and resources for teen girls and women. www.mydaughterskeeper.org or (732) 565-9313.

PLANNED PARENTHOOD, INC.: Provides access to sexual health information and local Planned Parenthood clinics. www.plannedparenthood.org or 1-800-230-PLAN.

SAFE HAVEN PROGRAM: Don't Abandon Your Baby! JUST DON'T DO IT! You can give up your baby safely, legally and anonymously at any hospital emergency room or police station. www.safehaven.org or 1-877-839-2339.

STAND UP GIRL: A support website for pregnant teen girls. www.standupgirl.com.

AMERICAN ADOPTIONS: Provides options for teenagers facing an unplanned pregnancy. www.americanadoptions.com or 1-800-ADOPTIONS.

LOCAL.COM: Provides links to pregnancy resources in your local community.

NATIONAL WOMEN'S HEALTH RESOURCE CENTER: Obtain questions and answers to ensure a healthy pregnancy. www.healthywomen.org or 1-877-986-9472.

NATIONAL CAMPAIGN TO PREVENT TEEN PREGNANCY: Access information and tips to prevent teen pregnancy. www.teenpregnancy.org or www.stayteen.org or 202-478-1500.

AMERICAN PREGNANCY ASSOCIATION: Promotes reproductive and pregnancy wellness through education, research, advocacy and community awareness resources. www.americanpregnancy.org or 1-800-672-2296.

Chapter Fourteen

LIKE MOTHER, LIKE DAUGHTER:
HOW DO OUR RELATIONSHIPS WITH OUR MOTHERS IMPACT HOW WE RAISE OUR CHILDREN?

In this chapter, several single moms speak candidly about their relationships with their mothers and how they feel their relationships impact how they raise their own children.

"My mom and I didn't have a very close relationship when I was growing up because she had three kids and a husband to take care of. She was a very good "homemaker" type of mom. My mom was always baking cookies, throwing big birthday parties, making Halloween costumes, hosting Halloween parties, and attending all school functions. My mom didn't talk to me too much about boys, sex, protection, going to college, etc. when I was younger (that I remember). I don't blame my mom for becoming a single mom; however, I feel that if I had more of a role-model and was led in the right direction I probably would not have been a single mom. Knowing all of that, I try to teach my daughter everything there is to know about life because I didn't get that from my mom growing up. Sometimes, I push my daughter too hard and try to stuff everything into her little brain about boys, drugs, sex, etc. because of what I felt I didn't get from my mom growing up."

Danielle Felder, California

"After God, my mother is my life force. She reminds me of every area where I could be failing but instead am succeeding. She reminds me to enjoy today because I won't get it back; we can't fight against time and win standing still in the center of a hectic whirlwind (life), she grounds me. I find myself saying some things that I never thought I would. She would always tell me, 'Danlia, no te aoges en un vaso de agua; don't drown in a glass of water - everyday will bring its own concerns.' When my children are all screaming at the same time for milk, toys or just attention, I remind myself that the water is only up to ankles - no need to believe I'm going to drown."

Danlia Reyes, New York

"My relationship with my mother is so much better since I became a mother. When I was growing up, I thought my mother was too passive, always ready and willing to help others. When I became a mother, I saw that quality in me and now in my daughter and I have to say I love it."

Darlene Morgan, New York

"Although my mother was addicted and I followed in her

footsteps, I am now drug-free and able to show my kids that I love them and will support them no matter what decisions they make. This is extremely important to me because I didn't have any support. But the one thing I could thank her for is being independent because regardless of her drug use she never let the child welfare system take us and she was a single mom as well."

Elsie Rivera, New Jersey

"My relationship with my mother is strained. However, I learned a lot of positive things from her for which I am grateful and that I have implemented in my own parenting style. There are things that I want to improve. One of which is my relationship with my children. I want to have an open and trusting relationship with them so that they are not afraid to tell me what is happening in their lives - good and bad alike. This is something that I do not have with my mother that I wish I did."

Faith McCalla, New Jersey

"Watching my mom work two and three jobs to provide for my brother and I made me appreciate her more. I learned from her that hard work pays off. She also taught us how to be independent. The same morals and values that she instilled in us, I try to instill in my girls. I didn't understand certain things as a child, teenager and young adult, but now I do and I know that she wasn't trying to make our lives miserable, she was trying to prepare us for the real world. I've always been very close to my mom. She was and still is always there for me, even if I make a mistake she's still there. She always encouraged me to talk to her and I always felt comfortable going to her with anything good or bad. She's the best."

Kasanu Sims, New Jersey

"Not having a good relationship with my mom has impacted my life as a mom today because I do things differently so my children can come to me and talk to me about everything. Whatever life throws at them I know that they can succeed through anything. I know she tried to do her best, but if her mother didn't talk to her, she was just repeating what was taught to her. So my challenge is to break the cycle and pave the way not only for my kids but also for my inheritance. There is a bond that you should always have with your mother no matter what, you only have one mother. I plan to instill great values in my children which I didn't receive, so my family won't be in bondage for the years to come."

Lakeya Crone, New Jersey

"It took a long time before I realized that my mother

internalized and that I'd also learned how to do that very well. I watched my mother who was a quiet woman and didn't know as a child what her quietness meant. I saw her beauty, grace, simplicity and strength as I watched my mother take care of her seven children -- dogmatically managing and making our house a beautiful home while often working part-time outside of the home. My mother was consistent with us and she worked very hard. I've taken on these traits and while I live a different lifestyle because I've always worked full-time outside of the home, these are qualities that I couldn't have succeeded without and would never trade."

Laticia Bailey, New Jersey

"My childhood was filled with domestic violence and assaults. My father knocked my mother around until she became an invalid. I was 8-years-old when my mother became an invalid. Eventually, my father murdered my mother and he later died in 1990. I was diagnosed before my mother's death with epilepsy due to my constant head smashing against brick walls, amongst other problems due to horrendous assaults. I then, like many others, married into it again and had my three kids. After my husband committed assaults, domestic violence and child abuse against me and my children, I got the courage to leave and divorce him. It took me a while to become a strong woman again and to undo the emotional damage that had been done to us. I thank my mother for giving me the background to be able to use it to my advantage to tackle the problems, which arose when I was in that situation and a mother myself."

Louise Marie Clayton, Wagga Wagga, Australia

"Self-esteem and maturity are essential to being a productive parent. Always seek a higher being for guidance and things will fall into place. My relationship with my mother has greatly impacted my life as a mom. My mother showed me how NOT to be a mother. She was the exact opposite of me and I vowed never to be like her. I don't know if my parenting skills are innovative or if I try very, very hard to do the opposite of what she did. My mother thinks she is my daughter. For a very long time my mother was jealous of my daughter and me, for that matter. I think that is very sad. I want to be the absolute best for my daughter. I want her to be a million times better than me and I want the same for her children. I would never want to be jealous of her. I want to always be proud of her. I would really be sad if my daughter didn't reach her full potential. I'll be there to support her no matter how far she surpasses me. I wish I could say that about my mom. She thinks my success is for her and she likes to brag about me but loves to berate me. The bragging part is about her."

Lynnette Caldwell, New Jersey

"My mother died when I was young so she was not really present physically but spiritually she is always there. Not having her to go to has made me more aware of how important that resource is for my daughters. I think I push more often than not for my daughter to come and talk to me about things that would naturally be a no-no, because I missed that opportunity as a daughter. I want to groom her because I missed being groomed by my mother."

Makeda Hunter, New Jersey

"My mother chose not to be a single parent and her decision has left me scarred, but not broken. I look at my daughter and I do not understand my mother's decision. For me, I know love is a choice that I make over and over every day. I wake my grumpy girl up with a smile every day. I give her some latitude for disagreement. I tell her I love her every day. I check her homework, ask her about her day, "nag" her all the time about the television shows I hate because she likes them and still tuck her in every night. She leaves the light on waiting for me. So even though I get the sullen, teenage attitude, she knows I am there for her no matter what."

Miriam Parrotto, New Jersey

"My mom died in 1982. It was one of the saddest events in my life. I never thought I would live a full and happy life after losing her. It took years to accept her death. Since then I have learned to take all the good that she was and apply it to my life. My mom was a strong and determined woman of faith. Her strength, her creativity, her love for mankind and her passion lives in me. I attribute all of my successes and accomplishments to my mother. I miss her so much in my life. I know her spirit continues to guide and teach me in many ways. I am who I am because of my mother."

Missouri, New Jersey

"My mother is GREAT, but when growing up it was so hard for me to talk to my mother. I was always compared to my sister because she was the straight A student who never got into any trouble. I hated that I was compared to my sister and others, so I always promised myself that if I had children I would never compare them and I would always let my children know they can talk to me about anything. I try my best not to compare my daughter to others. I always tell her to be her own person and that she's a leader!!!"

Natasha Taylor, New Jersey

"My mother gave me a card after the birth of my first daughter four years ago (I still have it) and it illustrated to me exactly how she felt about my becoming a mother. She is proud of me for choosing motherhood, thankful for allowing her to become part of the process, and hopeful that one day all of my dreams for my family and me will come true. We have been much closer since I have become a mother and she has become a grandmother, we talk on the phone everyday and communication between us has improved."

Nichole Harris, Maryland

"Since I was not raised by my biological mother, but raised by foster parents, I realize how important it is to be in my children's life as opposed to having someone else raise them. I also know how important it is to let my children know that I love them and how much I want them to be a part of my life. I have also been impacted from knowing how important it is to be open and honest with my daughters and not to keep secrets."

Robyn Lynn Blocker, New Jersey

"I didn't have a really close relationship with my mother. She was raised by her grandmother and didn't have a great relationship with her mother. My mother had me at 17 and already had my brother at 15. She was living on her own in

Bronx, NY. So as I was growing as an adolescent and teen, there were things that I needed that she spiritually, financially and physically wasn't able to give me. As a result, my daughter and I have a closer relationship because that is something that stayed with me and I didn't want my daughter to feel the way I felt so many times. I had low self-esteem and no one to reassure me or build me up. My mom was busy growing up into a young lady herself and working to try to provide for her children."

Shanick Moore, New Jersey

"My mother and father were married for the wrong reasons. They had so much hate in their hearts for one another that it caused our family to break up. My mother raised us for a long time by herself, and then my father raised us for the vital years of our lives, teenage years. My mother wasn't there when I had my first encounter with my menstrual cycle. She wasn't there when I needed to talk about why boys didn't like me, she wasn't there when I needed her to just sit with and talk about nonsense and she wasn't there for my teenage years. She has been there for my prom (she visited to see me off, but did not help with the dress, hair, nails, make-up...), first pregnancy, marriage and my second pregnancy, college graduation and most of what goes on in my life now. Teenage years for males and females are the most important. This is the time when you learn how to apply for college, how to love, how to earn money, how to save money, how to pick your career, how to know if that career isn't right for you and all of the major events in your life as a female. So, I'll say my relationship with my mother has impacted my life as a mom by helping me to see what I have to do for my girls in order for them to be successful and to have a better life spiritually, mentally, physically and financially. All of the things that I've missed out on during my vital years will sure be there for my girls during theirs."

Anonymous

"My relationship with my mother has impacted me everyday to be more unlike her in every way. Don't misunderstand the statement, I truly love my mother but, my father was more of a mother to me then my mother. Yes, we all lived in the same household but my mother was never really a mother. I do understand now and accept that in my life, because my mother lost both of her parents at a very young age. I strive to be closer with my daughters, listen more and talk less, hug and kiss every chance I get and say I love you as many times a day as I can. My relationship with my mother has shown me that the sky is the limit in motherhood and I am trying in every way to reach that limit and to go beyond with my children."

Tracey Slaughter, New Jersey

"I had my mom for a short 24 years of my life and our relationship impacted my parenting skills significantly. I had to raise a sister eight-years my junior when our mom passed suddenly from an asthma attack. The bond that was shared between me and my mother allows me to share our history with my daughter. My daughter may not have known her grandmother physically, but she is most definitely aware of her spirit. My mother's sense of self and fearlessness is passed onto another generation."

TJ Dupree, New Jersey

Chapter Fifteen

WE HAVE COME THIS FAR BY OUR FAITH

As I read through the stories submitted by the Single Moms who contributed their stories to this book, I was humbled and honored to know that I am in the company of so many spirit-filled women. It soon became evident while reading their stories that many of the single moms, including myself, rely heavily on their faith to get them through the many challenges that they have faced as both a woman and single mom.

I can personally witness that my faith has gotten me through many trials and tribulations. It is my faith on which I stand firm and steadfast. For I know, as well as many of my single mom contributors, that it is our faith in God that has brought us thus far and has enabled us to raise our children on our own.

During our dark hours, lonely nights, and when we feel that we are carrying the weight of the world on our shoulders, it is our faith that gives us hope, strength and determination to weather the storms that come our way.

It is our faith that reminds us, when we are confronted with situations that seem bleak and too heavy a burden to carry on our own, that we are not alone.

It is our faith that assures us that we are not forsaken nor forgotten especially during times like these:

- ❖ Our employers lay us off from our jobs unexpectedly;
- ❖ Our rent or mortgage is three months past due;
- ❖ Our children are being defiant and acting up;
- ❖ Our relationships with the men in our life just do not seem to work out;
- ❖ There seems to be more bills and less money to pay them;
- ❖ We are experiencing all types of health challenges; and
- ❖ We just cannot seem to get ahead.

It is our faith that confirms that through Jesus Christ all things are possible and that we are more than conquerors for we are women who truly love the Lord. It is through our faith that we can celebrate times like these:

- ❖ When despite the odds and statistics, we are raising healthy, productive children;
- ❖ When God sends us financial blessings that come just in time!;
- ❖ When God places people in our lives to be blessings to us;
- ❖ When we know that we are never alone and that there are others who are walking in our shoes who will share our joys and our pains;
- ❖ When God touches us with His healing power;

❖ When God opens doors and provides opportunities we never knew existed;

❖ When God grants us the desires of our hearts;

❖ When God makes our enemies our footstools;

❖ When God hears our cries in the midnight hour and wipes away our tears; and

❖ When God makes us feel that He is the most important man that we need in our lives.

Chapter Sixteen

WORDS OF WISDOM BY SINGLE MOMS FOR SINGLE MOMS

"Today, I realize that single parenting is not an impossible journey as long as you rely on God and ask Him to guide your life. He will send you "comfort" through people, places and things if you ask Him. My words of wisdom are that only when you commit yourself to persevere no matter what the dilemma: illness, stress, lack - you can endure single parenting with or without family support. You should always remember God is with you so you are not alone. You can turn anything into a positive if you never give in or give up."

Anita Yasin, New Jersey

"My advice to other single moms is to make time for you so that you don't lose yourself in being the number one caretaker for the children. As a single mother, I always planned my time around the children. In today's society, I see a host of single moms passing the responsibility of caring for their children off to the grandparents."

Betty Williams, New Jersey

"To other single moms I say, "You can do it!" It is hard and there are times you feel like you are faced with so many obstacles, but you look at your child and know your purpose here is to ensure their life's dreams."

Carla Alexander, New Jersey

"It takes a lot of sacrifice, prayer and hard work but if you have a dream for yourself, you are supporting the dream of your children by believing that anything is possible. If you want to go back to school, start your own business, whatever it is, it can be done. Also know that our children are a product of their environment. Remember your children are watching and learning from the most important person in their life and that is you."

Cassandra White Graves, Ohio

"You are embarking on one of the greatest challenges of your life. Instead of feeling resentful about being a single mom and all of the challenges you face on a daily basis, embrace the fact that you cannot only survive as a single parent, but thrive. Focus your thoughts on all of the benefits-my favorite is having my king size bed all to myself without a snoring husband in it and all of the extra closet and drawer space!"

Christina Rowe, Florida

"Don't let anyone tell you that you can't make it in life, despite your past. Go after everything your heart desires and have faith in what YOU believe in, not what society tells you to believe in.

Surround yourself with positive, motivated, and inspirational people. Stay away from negative, drama-filled, jealous or envious people. If it sounds too good to be true (and legal), 99.9% of the time it is. Single moms can fulfill their dreams and goals in life, just as good (if not better) than anyone else. Life is what you make it. If you're going through something right now and you feel there's no light at the end of the tunnel, you're wrong. There is always light at the end and the sun will shine again. I've been there; I've experienced financial heartache, loss of close family and friends, loneliness, loss of jobs and home, car theft, emotional distress, physical and verbal abuse from ex-boyfriends, parental abandonment, etc. If I can make it through all of that and still have faith, then so can you."

Danielle Felder, California

"My advice to other single moms is to BREATHE!!!! Seems like something silly to say but in the midst of sewing on buttons, keeping a job, cooking, cleaning, bathing, cleaning some more, wiping tears, helping with homework and remembering that you haven't showered - the simple act of breathing - just taking a second to catch your breath is forgotten. Realizing that the world isn't going to fall apart because you left a dish in the sink or your toddler refused to go to sleep without his new sneakers on or maybe your teenage daughter wants you to meet a 'friend.' Look in the mirror, pat yourself on the back, and say 'You're doing a good job.' If you don't believe it in your mind then you won't reflect it in your actions. Truly humbling yet affirming!"

Danlia Reyes, New York

"My advice to other single mothers is don't believe that you are a statistic. Just because you are raising a child by yourself does not mean you cannot accomplish your goals and live a good life. Go back to school and get that degree you always wanted. Take up a hobby and treasure your time doing it."

Darlene Morgan, New York

"Cherish moments and make your moments with children. Enjoy the special bond. Have a spiritual side and believe in a higher power. My aid was God. Do not forget you exist and you need to take care of yourself spiritually, mentally and physically to be able to handle all the rough times in life. At the end of the day being a parent is hearing your own inner voice and trusting your instincts."

Elizabeth Lopez, New Jersey

"What I know for sure today as a single mom is to keep a close friend who isn't judgmental about your circumstance, but holds you accountable when you just feel like you can't take it anymore. This person ideally would allow you to vent when you need to. Educate yourself and get involved in a support group.

I had to learn quickly that the battle is not mine, it is truly the Lord's!"

Gayle Nelson, PhD, New Jersey

"Being a single parent is not easy and without God in your life, it is literally impossible. I believe that I do my best in most everything that I try. I have learned to take parenting one day at a time. Parenting takes time and practice; children are not born with a manual. You will need to learn that boys and girls are not the same and how to address their individual needs."

Glynis F. Sanders, New Jersey

"When it seems too much to bear, dig deeper inside yourself and reach out for support. "No woman is an island." Know that many have done it before you, and you are not alone."

Jeanine Fuller, Tennessee

"In the divorce process, don't give up the alimony, no matter how much money you think you can earn! I waived that knowing that I am capable of earning money, given my education and skills. However, after a divorce, it takes a while to get back on your feet. Things come up that are unexpected and I would feel more comfortable if I hadn't given up that financial assistance. Also, don't be scared to ask for help."

Kelley Nayo, California

"For other single mothers, I say love yourself and accept who you are; but make changes to become far better than who you are today. Live life as if it is your last chance and enjoy the time with your child or children. Raise your children to become leaders of the world and live your life as a great role-model. Take responsibility, forgive and enjoy your life with peace and; more importantly, lend a helping hand especially to single mothers because what you give out will come back with shine. Single moms should know that protecting your child or children from those who will place you in a difficult situation should not be ignored. Take responsibility to put your children first and foremost and accept no less than that. There are often times we as women will put other things and people before the very people who need us the most. Our children are the future generation and as single mothers we must look out for the welfare of our children and not allow them to become another statistic by becoming institutionalized or the responsibility of the child welfare system."

La-trenda Ross, New Jersey

"I think it is important to find joy and happiness in the simple things, no matter what you have. It is also important to maintain balance in your life and find time for yourself as a woman. I think it is important for single moms to know that your children have to love both parents. Children should not feel the need to choose between their parents.

It doesn't matter what he thinks or they think, what matters is how you think and feel about yourself! Empower yourself, through reading, meditation, exercise and loving you...love YOU FIRST!!! Lose the stuff that weighs you down, if it does not fit, drop it and move forward!!! Depend on GOD and YOU!!!! Find a way to give back. Get involved with organizations that touch you, that speak to your passion or start one yourself. LIVE YOUR PASSION NOW!!!"

Miriam Parrotto, New Jersey

"I know there are days where you feel like you can't do anymore, because God knows I have been there. But God will never give us more than what we can handle. It's unfortunate that we have to do this alone, but there is a purpose for our lives."

Natasha Taylor, New Jersey

"I have learned that all I have to do is PRAY and have faith! Prayer will empower me and faith will keep me going. Life is not void of challenges and obstacles, however, it's much easier to overcome obstacles when one stays in prayer."

Nichole Harris, New Jersey

"Don't get caught up in life's hustle and bustle and miss the important years of your children's lives. Ask for help as much as possible - when needed. Make sure that the fathers of our daughters take an active role in their lives if it's not a harmful or an immoral environment."

Robyn Lynn Blocker, New Jersey

"Parenting is so serious that words can't really express the love and constant concern a parent has. Parenting is something that you should get into when you are ready spiritually (leading them the proper way), financially (being able to provide for them), physically (are you physically capable of keeping up with a child, your health is in order), and mentally (being able to let go of past hurts and issues to be able to raise a well-nurtured, secure child). There's so much to think about before making such a life altering decision."

Shanick Moore, New Jersey

"My advice for other single mothers is to realize that while you are rearing a child, they are growing up. As a parent, we should not stop growing either. Sometimes, parents become so engulfed in bringing up their child that when the child becomes an adult they are lost from not preparing for that day. I knew that I could not pursue some dreams while I was a teen mom but the moment they got old enough, I started to go after them. I took singing classes that led to my singing at weddings. I took a role in a musical. I contracted for a one-day gig singing at IKEA during the holidays. I started my own small business. Our children go on with their lives, so we have to ensure that as parents we have lives of our own."

Simone Bellamy, New Jersey

"My advice to other single moms is to reach out to as many healthy people (support groups, organizations, church, etc.) to help be a support in any way. Network, use the phone. Believe in your dreams. No pity parties. No laziness or ungrateful attitudes - they gotta go. Strengthen your entire being and tap into your talents. Use your experience to empower yourself for your children. Let your pain be turned into ammunition (ammo) to develop a happy successful life. If I can do it, you can do it."

Sinneh Rose, Massachusetts

"What I know for sure today as a single mom is that I'm happy and that life throws many curves that you must adjust to. I know for sure that it's not the end of the world to be alone and that if the trials you experience don't kill you, they will definitely make you stronger.

It's not easy being a single mom but it's not the end of the world either. Take one day at a time and don't be so serious about the unnecessary evils that life can toss at you."

Tracie Rasberry, Michigan

"As single mothers, we must stay focused on our individual goals while incorporating and uplifting our children at the same time. We must be conscious of leaving a legacy in place."

TJ Dupree, New Jersey

Chapter Seventeen

WORDS OF WISDOM FROM SINGLE MOMS TO OUR DAUGHTERS

"I admonish my daughters to wait until they are ready for children. Parenting is so much easier when there are two parents."

Acquanetta King, New Jersey

"I would encourage my daughter to always tell her children how much she loves them. Never say goodbye or goodnight without saying I love you; always hug them and let them know how much they mean to you because you do not know what tomorrow brings."

Amy Carlton, New Jersey

"I had two children out of wedlock and never married so I always encourage my children to wait until they are married to have children. Get your college degrees, travel, have fun and then, when the time is right, get married and plan the family."

Betty Williams, New Jersey

"Having a family is a wonderful part of life; but before you make the decision to start a family, make sure the following decisions are made: Are you educated and skilled enough to provide for a family? Can you provide food, a home, clothing, insurance, transportation, daycare, health care and education for yourself and your child? If you answer no to any one of these questions, you need to put yourself in a position where you can provide. If you answered yes and are dating, you need to ask yourself some important questions regarding the person you will choose for a partner. Can the potential mate answer yes to all the above questions? If his answers are yes, your second set of questions should be: does he have children with another woman? Does he take excellent care of his children? Is he active in his children's life on a consistent, everyday basis whether or not they are now adult children? Is he an abuser or addicted to any drugs or alcohol? Does he have any mental problems?"

Cassandra White Graves, Ohio

"Please, please, please...wait until you have finished college and traveled the world to see what else life has to offer before even thinking about being a parent. Parenting is hard and takes a lot of dedication, but it is a beautiful thing. Marriage is also beautiful (so I've been told because I haven't been married yet). Get married before deciding to have kids. Live your life first because once you have kids, your life is centered around their life. I don't recommend following in my footsteps and becoming a teenage mother."

Danielle Felder, California

"Some life lessons I have learned are that I am not alone; my life is equally important; a plan is a necessity; and how to say "no." Single mothers must learn to say "no," "wait," and "I'm sorry." Being a single mother is not an excuse for failure."

Julie Dennis, New Jersey

"I would like my daughter to "realize that you are not a superwoman so don't try to be!" You will never be able to do and give everything. Just do what is right, do what you can, and love with all your heart. Take time for yourself. If you don't take time to work on yourself as a person, you will soon find out that you have nothing left to give to your children. Have faith in God and know that he will guide and carry you through your hardest days and darkest nights."

Monique Lawton, New Jersey

"I attempt to instill in my children not to bring children into this world unless they are willing to make the sacrifices it will take to raise them, even if you have to do it alone!"

Pamela Vail, New Jersey

"The wisdom that I would share with my daughter is to be patient and wait for a mate that supports and compliments her as a person for this is the best recipe for rearing a happy, productive child."

Simone Bellamy, New Jersey

Chapter Eighteen

SINGLE MOM SUCCESS STORIES IF THEY CAN DO IT; YOU CAN DO IT!

"My accomplishments, as I see it, included my son getting into college and now graduating. My mother and I developed a loving relationship and I was able to bond with her despite her childhood. My daughter is studying to be a teen minister and is facing her mental illness through prayer and perseverance. I have two beautiful children whom I challenged to fight back against their own obstacles. My only wish, had I known what I now know, would be that I stopped feeling isolated earlier and recognized the power of the Lord to strengthen me more often. I learned late to pray over my kids and situations that were not God's will. I wish I had known that I only needed to ask Him to intercede for me."

Anita Yasin, New Jersey

"My greatest accomplishments as a single mom are going back to college and receiving my Associate Degree, currently pursuing my Bachelor of Science Degree and maintaining a loving home for my children. Besides the absence of another parent, my children have reaped more benefits than children that do have both parents available. Another great accomplishment for me was seeing my daughter on the honor roll after being labeled as having a learning disability. She has now been on the honor roll for two years straight!"

Charisse Roberts, New Jersey

"Deeply in debt but feeling as though a huge weight had been lifted off my shoulders; I began to rebuild my life both financially and emotionally. During this time I began to think about all of the other women who might be going through a similar situation. I wanted to help other women avoid the pitfalls of divorce and teach them the survival skills they needed to have a positive divorce outcome.

I began to take the knowledge I had learned during my divorce and decided to write a book about my experience. "Seven Secrets to a Successful Divorce - What Every Woman Needs to Know" was published almost three years to the day I separated from my husband.

I believe everything in life happens for a reason. Divorce taught me, and now it's my turn to teach others. I made it through the storm. I discovered my inner strength and have become a stronger, happier woman."

Christina Rowe, Florida

"My greatest accomplishments as a single mom are being able to reach my goals when I thought I would be nothing but a failure (and was told this by friends and family members) because of my 'teenage mom' and 'drug dealer boyfriends' background. Thinking I would never be able to go to college because I didn't have money and my parents couldn't afford to send me. By the grace of God and a lot of hard work, determination, and motivation, I was able to receive my A.A. Degree, B.S. Degree and Master's Degree...graduating with a 3.9 GPA, while working and being a full-time mom. I became a homeowner in Oct. 2004. I opened my own business in Apr. 2006. I landed a HR Mgmt. position in Oct. 2006 with a great company making over $65k salary. Being able to be my daughter's role-model, keep her on the straight and narrow and focused on her educational goals are great accomplishments. My daughter is a straight A student, ranking #7 out of 334 students at her school. Despite not having a father, she is an excellent, well-mannered child, with a passion for learning and is loved by everyone (including all her teachers). I have myself (and God) to thank for that."

Danielle Felder, California

"My greatest accomplishments as a single mom are obtaining a Bachelor's Degree, working full-time and giving my son adequate care full-time. I've managed to obtain my degree within three years as well as shape my son into a well-mannered, successful student. Living with the knowledge that my son will be able to say, "My Mommy went to college and I will do the same," is what makes being his mom worth all the challenges."

Deborah Morillo, New York

"Inviting God into my life was a way of finding my way to happiness and bringing joy to me and my family. I had a terrible habit indulging in illegal drugs that had captured my soul. I once was lost but now I am found; standing to face all challenges and having the confidence in myself that I never had before. I have learned to empower myself to become independent and gain control of my life in order to make decisions that are healthy for my family and myself. I have accomplished earning an Applied Associate Degree in Human Services, employed with a powerful non-profit organization, saving towards the future, currently earning my Bachelors Degree in Psychology and searching to purchase a home for the first time. I am elated to have both of my daughters graduate with their high school diplomas and to see them live their lives independently. I have overcome a battle that some single mothers are trapped in now such as drugs, alcohol, domestic violence, and low self-esteem. I have been substance abuse free for over fifteen years and today I have chosen to live a spiritual and clean life for my children and myself. I believe in myself and the goodness in others; and feel good about life knowing that I am somebody. I can live a life without the intoxicated filth that can hurt and destroy my life. Some people wonder how someone can overcome drugs and alcohol; and I say it is my higher power who is God."

La-trenda, Ross, New Jersey

"I am a very proud mother. I have raised three productive and successful young men and my daughter will be graduating from high school in 2008 and going into college, majoring in Performing Arts. It has been a challenging road of growing and learning. Some of my greatest accomplishments are being able to remain focused on my dreams and passions while assisting and empowering my children in pursuing theirs. I have truly beat the odds. According to society, I am not supposed to be where I am today. I have overcome many obstacles and still I rise. I am thankful for all the angels that have come my way to shine their light. My goal is to position myself to be a better person daily and to continue on my journey of unconditional love and empowerment. Starting a non-profit, Celebration Of Life Awards (C.O.L.A.) is my greatest accomplishment. I truly believe everything I have done in my life was preparing me for

C.O.L.A.; this is why I was brought here. I now know my purpose, what a great feeling and what a great accomplishment!!!!"

Missouri, New Jersey

"When I tell myself I want something, I ask God if it is in my best interest and I pray for His support, and He makes it happen! After leaving my daughter's father two years ago, I hoped to find a roommate with similar morals and values, someone who I could trust. God showed me and for almost two years, I have been living with a 34-year-old single mother. She is the greatest person! We wanted to find a nicer home than our first town-home. So I prayed. We applied for a few homes and received the one we wanted. Additionally, I wanted to re-enroll in graduate school. So, last summer I prayed for acceptance back into the program. I began classes in Sept 2006! After enrolling in school, I knew I would need a job with a more flexible schedule. After applying for hundreds of jobs and after praying for months, I found a position in a different department, closer to both campus and to my home. I prayed for God to bring a God-fearing man into my life who I can grow and share in the joy of the Lord with. I asked for a sensitive, honest, caring, hard-working, intelligent, independent man with "minimal drama." James and I became official on Mothers Day! GOD is good!"

Nichole Harris, Maryland

INDEX OF SINGLE MOM STORIES

*NOTE: Single mom stories appear throughout chapters, however, for privacy purposes, names are not included with stories that share very private and personal details.

ABOUT THE AUTHOR...

Stephanie M. Clark is a native of Detroit. She received her Bachelor of Science degree in Business Administration and Marketing from the University of Detroit-Mercy in 1991. In 1999, she completed an accelerated program, Nonprofit Marketing and Management, from Fordham University in New York City. She has worked in Marketing for over 15 years in the areas of Public Relations, Media Relations, Event Management, Advertising, Sales and Management. Ms. Clark worked for two nonprofit organizations over an eight-year period in the roles of Marketing & PR Director for the Museum of African American History in Detroit, MI and Marketing & Sales Director for Crossroads Theatre Company in New Brunswick, NJ. She has also consulted for several local and national faith-based, non-profit organizations and corporations as a marketing communications consultant. She has traveled abroad as a publicist for internationally known clients as well as throughout the United States planning multi-day conferences for national associations.

Inspired by her daughter Daphne, and her mother who raised 13 children as a single mother, Clark founded My Daughter's Keeper, Inc. (MDK) in July 2002. MDK is a 501(c)(3) multi-cultural nonprofit organization which provides support and resources to mothers and caregivers raising adolescent and teenage daughters as well as provides self-development opportunities for women and girls. MDK works with mothers/caregivers and their daughters, women and girls from all socioeconomic backgrounds.

Ms. Clark has received several awards on behalf of My Daughter's Keeper's public service including the prestigious Women as Agents of Change Award for 2003 from the American Association of University Women. She was one of three women chosen to receive the honor representing Central New Jersey. She also received the 2004 Central Jersey Women Who Make Magic Award; the 2004 Charming Shoppes VOICES Award (a national recognition); the 2004 Nu Xi Omega Chapter of AKA Sorority, Inc. P.E.A.R.L. Award for the Black Family; the 2004 Russ Berrie Unsung Hero Award; the 2006 BlackNJ Community Commitment Award; the 2006 KISS-98.7FM Radio "Phenomenal Woman" Award; 2006 "Outstanding Contribution to Empowering Women" Award from Trinity Chapter Order of Eastern Star; and the 2006 Celebration of Life Award.

She serves on the Board of Directors for the Women's Fund of New Jersey. Ms. Clark is a Leadership Newark Fellow, Class of 2005. She serves on the Juvenile Justice Delinquency Prevention's Young Women Action Agenda Sub-committee for the New Jersey Juvenile Justice Commission, the Middlesex County Youth Council, and the New Brunswick Tomorrow Youth Task Force.

Ms. Clark is frequently sought out to serve as a motivational and keynote speaker as well as a workshop facilitator for groups serving women and girls throughout the tri-state area. "Life As A Single Mom: It Isn't Easy of Is It?" is Clark's debut book. She is also writing a book on how to start a non-profit business and a character building workbook for teens. Both books to be published by MDK Media, Inc. (a for-profit subsidiary of My Daughter's Keeper, Inc.) are scheduled for release in 2008. She resides in Central New Jersey with her daughter.

ABOUT MY DAUGHTER'S KEEPER...

Founded in 2002, My Daughter's Keeper, Inc. (MDK) is a national, 501(c)(3) educational and self-development non-profit organization, based in Central New Jersey, created to provide support and resources to mothers/caregivers and daughters (ages 8-19) to help strengthen individuals, families and communities. In addition, MDK provides self-development opportunities for women and girls to improve their quality of life.

MDK promotes parental accountability and works to encourage and empower mothers/caregivers to accept and take responsibility for raising their daughters to become productive, confident, and self-respecting young ladies. Our goal is to help develop our daughters into women equipped with the proper morals and values to empower and prepare them to pursue their dreams and goals. Ultimately, they will take and use what has been instilled in them to make a positive impact in their communities and society at large.

MDK will launch the following affiliates during 2007-2008: My Daughter's Keeper of Greater Paterson, NJ (launched Sept 07); My Daughter's Keeper of Tampa Bay, FL (launched Nov 07); My Daughter's Keeper of New Brunswick, NJ (2007); My Daughter's Keeper of Newark, NJ (2008); My Daughter's Keeper of Bergen County, NJ (2008); and My Daughter's Keeper of Detroit, MI (2008). Learn more at www.mydaughterskeeper.org

ABOUT MDK MEDIA, INC....

MDK Media, Inc. is a social enterprise subsidiary established as a for-profit business in 2005 to generate earned income to help sustain and further the mission of My Daughter's Keeper, Inc. (MDK), the parent nonprofit organization. MDK Media, Inc. also referred to as MDK Worldwide, Inc. provides publishing, media relations, and training and development services to aspiring and published authors as well as aspiring and new business (for-profit and not-for-profit) visionaries. MDK Media seeks to empower women and girls to become published authors, trained media professionals, and entrepreneurs as a means to obtaining self-sufficiency and enhancing their quality of life by putting their financial futures in their own hands.

MDK Media, Inc. also provides a speaker's bureau comprised of a diverse group of women and girls of color empowered and equipped to provide inspiring keynote addresses, motivational speeches, book signings, and interactive and lively workshops for various groups; including women/girls groups and organizations, churches, corporations, professional associations, schools and universities. Learn more at www.mdkmediainc.com.

ABOUT PROJECT SINGLE MOMS...

PROJECT SINGLE MOMS™ (PSM) is a program of My Daughter's Keeper Worldwide created as an international movement designed to empower, educate, engage, energize, equip and enhance the quality of life for single mothers.

PSM PHILOSOPHY

PSM is first about you, the Woman, and secondly about you, the Mother. It is about learning how to put your needs first and all others second. We have defined this action as Heart Reversal™ which is simply turning your heart inward to give back to yourself. It is about taking time to make time for you. When you become a more fulfilled, productive woman, you can then raise fulfilled, productive children. When you are healthy and happy, your children will be healthy and happy. It is okay to love yourself more.

PROJECT SINGLE MOMS
It's About a Hand Up, Not a Hand Out

PSM OBJECTIVES

➢ To empower single moms to pursue their dreams and passions by challenging them to step outside of their comfort zones to live their best life ever.

➢ To educate single moms by connecting them to resources to help make better informed and wiser choices for their lives.

➢ To engage single moms to connect with other single moms, and seek opportunities to help themselves by helping others.

➢ To energize single moms to take action and make things happen in their lives.

➢ To equip single moms with information, tools, and access to people and opportunities to help them accomplish their personal and professional goals.

➢ To enhance the perspectives of single moms that, through focused-efforts and hard work, they can live the life they have always imagined.

Learn more at www. projectsinglemoms.com

ABOUT A HAND UP FUND...
NOWHERE TO TURN? TURN TO US!

A Hand Up Fund™ offers temporary financial assistance to Single Moms for emergency and empowerment purposes without an obligation to repay. The fund dollars are created through annual memberships and personal donations of single moms and other contributors. In addition, annual fundraising activities will help sustain the growth of the fund. The fund anticipates helping a minimum of 20 single moms in its first year. The fund will support single moms both nationally and internationally.

The fund's philosophy is to "Pay it Forward" and encourages single moms who are helped through the fund to help other single moms by contributing back into the fund or providing direct assistance to a single mom.

100% OF BOOK SALES WILL SUPPORT THE MISSION AND PROGRAMS OF MY DAUGHTER'S KEEPER, INC. TWENTY-FIVE PERCENT (25%) OF ALL BOOK SALES WILL GO TOWARDS CREATING AND SUSTAINING "A HAND UP FUND."

To find out if you are eligible to apply for assistance, visit www.projectsinglemoms.com.

PROJECT SINGLE MOMS
It's About a Hand Up, Not a Hand Out

1000 SINGLE MOMS
MEMBERSHIP CHALLENGE

Help Us Help You. We need 1,000 single moms to become a member of Project Single Moms by December 31, 2008 to help build and maintain "A Hand Up" Fund to support single mothers around the world, and to officially launch the fund to begin granting requests on January 1, 2008.

We all need help at some point in our lives and sometimes we do not know who or where to turn to for help to get over a hump, or to help move our dream forward.

A Hand Up Fund may be just the assistance you need just in time.

Go to www.projectsinglemoms.com to learn more about the wonderful benefits of membership with Project Single Moms. Then, tell every single mother you know to join and enjoy the incentives. We are all in this together!

PROJECT SINGLE MOMS DEMOGRAPHICS:

We thought you may be interested in learning more about the 47 Project Single Moms who participated in this book project.

AGE:

2%	19 - 25 years old
14%	26 - 30 years old
20%	31 - 35 years old
20%	36 - 40 years old
24%	41 - 45 years old
16%	46 - 50 years old
4%	+50 years old

EMPLOYMENT:

64%	Employed
17%	Self Employed
13%	Homemakers
6%	Unemployed

Note: Although over 50% of the PSM are employed, over 50% would like to pursue self-employment opportunities.

ANNUAL INCOME:

11%	Earn between Less than $20K
49%	Earn between $21-$50K
38%	Earn between $51-$99K
2%	Earn above $100K

Note: Only one PSM earned above $100K.

EDUCATION:

43%	Earned GED/High School Diploma
11%	Earned Associate's Degree
23%	Earned Bachelor's Degree
23%	Earned Master's Degree

Note: More than 50% of PSM desire to complete and obtain advanced degrees.

ETHNICITY:

75%	African American
12%	Hispanic
11%	Caucasian
2%	Other

Note: Three-fourths of PSM respondents are African American single moms.

NUMBER OF CHILDREN:

25%	1 Child
38%	2 Children
27%	3 Children
8%	4 Children
2%	5 or More Children

LENGTH OF TIME AS A SINGLE MOM:

29%	1-5 Years
20%	5-10 Years
33%	10-15 Years
18%	+15 Years

Note: More single moms remain unmarried for a longer length of time and, most, not by choice.

HEALTH:

Has Medical Insurance:	88%	Yes
	12%	No
Has Life Insurance:	78%	Yes
	22%	No
Children Insured:	92%	Yes
	8%	No
Receives Child Support:	51%	Yes
	49%	No

THEIR NEEDS ACCORDING TO PRIORITY:

56%	Financial
44%	Parent Support
35%	Health & Wellness
33%	Education
27%	Spiritual
21%	Transportation
19%	Relationship
19%	Housing
9%	Employment
8%	Medical

If you would like to participate in this survey to help us understand the needs of single moms, please complete the online survey at:

www.projectsinglemoms.com

HOW TO BOOK A SPEAKER/BOOK SIGNING

If you are interested in booking Stephanie M. Clark as a speaker or workshop facilitator for your conference or event, contact the Speaker's Bureau at speakers@mdkmediainc.com to request a Speaker's Request Package.

If you would like to schedule a book signing with Ms. Clark and Project Single Moms™ Book Contributors, email us at contactus@projectsinglemoms.com

If you are interested in becoming a member of MDK Media Inc.'s National Speaker's Bureau, email us at speakers@mdkmediainc.com.

MDK MEDIA, INC.
1086 LIVINGSTON AVENUE, SUITE 4
NORTH BRUNSWICK, NJ 08902
PHONE: (732) 565-3793, EXT. 1
FAX: (732) 565-1019

HOW YOU CAN GET INVOLVED

✓ JOIN THE NATIONAL MOVEMENT TO EMPOWER MOTHERS AND DAUGHTERS AROUND THE WORLD. BECOME A MEMBER TODAY!
GO TO WWW.MYDAUGHTERSKEEPER.ORG

✓ JOIN THE INTERNATIONAL MOVEMENT TO EMPOWER SINGLE MOMS AROUND THE WORLD. BECOME A MEMBER TODAY!
GO TO WWW.PROJECTSINGLEMOMS.COM

✓ JOIN THE TRANSFORMING MINDS BY TRANSFORMING MEANINGS FOR TEENS NATIONAL CAMPAIGN
GO TO WWW.MDKMEDIAINC.COM

UPCOMING PROJECTS

Plan ahead and join us for these
upcoming events:

National Mother and Daughter
Holistic Health Retreat (2008)
Visit www.mydaughterskeeper.org for
New Jersey (Dates TBD)

International Single Moms Empowerment
Conference Cruise (2009)
Visit www.projectsinglemoms.com for
Caribbean (Dates TBD)

National Mother and Daughter
Holistic Health Retreat (2010)
Visit www.mydaughterskeeper.org or more info.
Tampa Bay, FL (Dates TBD)

HOW TO ORDER COPIES

I would like to order a copy or copies of the book "Life as a Single Mom: It Isn't Easy, Or Is It?":

Book Quantity:_____ @ $15.00 each/Total Costs: $_____

Fax Orders: (732) 565-1019/Telephone Orders: (732) 565-3793, ext. 8. Please have your credit card ready
Online Orders via credit card: Visit www.projectsinglemoms.com

Mail Orders: Project Single Moms™
              c/o MDK Media, Inc.
              1086 Livingston Avenue, Suite 4
              North Brunswick, NJ 08902

Ship to:_____

Address: _____

City: _____

State: _____ Zip Code:_____

Phone:_____

Email: _____

Shipping: $2.50 for each book shipped in U.S.
              $8.00 shipped outside U.S.
              $5.00 handling fee applied to each order.

Total Books Costs: $_____ plus S & H Costs: $_____

Payment Method: ❑ Check   ❑ Credit Card
Make Checks Payable to: MDK Media, Inc.

              ❑ Visa   ❑ Master Card   ❑ AmEx   ❑ Discover

Name on Card: _____

Billing Address: _____

City: _____State: _____Zip_____

Card Number:_____

Expiration Date:_____*CV Number_____

*Refer to 3 or 4 digit number on back or front (AmEx) of credit card

MDK Media, Inc.

Empowering and Enhancing
the Lives of Mothers & Daughters,
Women and Girls
Around the World

JOIN THE MOVEMENT TODAY!

100% OF BOOK SALE PROCEEDS WILL
SUPPORT THE MISSION AND PROGRAMS
OF MY DAUGHTER'S KEEPER, INC.